China Briefing

The Practical Application of China Business

For further volumes:
http://www.springer.com/series/8839
http://www.asiabriefingmedia.com

Dezan Shira & Associates is a specialist foreign direct investment practice, providing business advisory, tax, accounting, payroll and due diligence services to multinationals investing in China, Hong Kong, India and Vietnam. Established in 1992, the firm is a leading regional practice in Asia with seventeen offices in four jurisdictions, employing over 170 business advisory and tax professionals.

We also provide useful business information through our media and publishing house, Asia Briefing.

Chris Devonshire-Ellis · Andy Scott
Sam Woollard
Editors

Mergers & Acquisitions in China

Second Edition

 Springer   **DEZAN SHIRA & ASSOCIATES**

Editors
Chris Devonshire-Ellis
Andy Scott
Sam Woollard
Dezan Shira & Associates
Asia Briefing Ltd
Unit 1618, 16/F, Miramar Tower
132 Nathan Road
Tsim Sha Tsui, Kowloon
Hong Kong, People's Republic of China
e-mail: editor@asiabriefingmedia.com

ISBN 978-3-642-14918-4   e-ISBN 978-3-642-14919-1

DOI 10.1007/978-3-642-14919-1

Springer Heidelberg Dordrecht London New York

Library of Congress Control Number: 2010938286

Published by Springer-Verlag Berlin Heidelberg 2011
© Asia Briefing Ltd. 2008, 2011

This work is subject to copyright. All rights are reserved, whether the whole or part of the material is concerned, specifically the rights of translation, reprinting, reuse of illustrations, recitation, broadcasting, reproduction on microfilm or in any other way, and storage in data banks. Duplication of this publication or parts thereof is permitted only under the provisions of the German Copyright Law of September 9, 1965, in its current version, and permission for use must always be obtained from Springer. Violations are liable to prosecution under the German Copyright Law.

The use of general descriptive names, registered names, trademarks, etc. in this publication does not imply, even in the absence of a specific statement, that such names are exempt from the relevant protective laws and regulations and therefore free for general use.

Cover design: eStudio Calamar, Berlin/Figueres

Printed on acid-free paper

Springer is part of Springer Science+Business Media (www.springer.com)

About China Briefing's China Business Guides

Thank you for buying this book. *China Briefing*'s publications are designed to fill a niche in the provision of information about business law and tax in China. When we decided, several years ago, to commence this series, we did so in the knowledge that much that was available about China was either expensive, or completely contradictory. Plus much of it did not really adequately address the real issues faced by businessmen—the practical knowledge that must be part of any business dealings in developing countries. This guide is designed to change that perspective and provide detailed information and the regulatory background to business in China—but with a firm eye also on the details of making money and remaining in compliance.

Accordingly, we have made this guide informative, easy to read and inexpensive. To do so we have engaged not a team of journalists or academics—but the services of a respected professional services firm to assist us. The articles and materials within have been researched and written by China-based Chinese and international lawyers, accountants and auditors, familiar with the issues that foreign invested enterprises face in China—as they service them in China as clients. These professionals have come from the nationally established practice, Dezan Shira & Associates, and we are grateful for their support. Without them this book would not have been possible, and we wholeheartedly recommend their services should you require sensible and pragmatic advice as contained within this book.

At *China Briefing*, our motto is "The practical application of China business" and we hope that within this volume and our other publications you feel we have achieved this, and helped point you in the right direction when it comes to understanding and researching this vast and complicated business environment.

Asia Briefing Publications
Hong Kong

Contents

M&A Environment in China	1
Chinese Legislation on M&A	9
Structuring Your Own Mergers and Acquisitions	29
Acquisition	33
Due Diligence	37
Valuing an Acquisition Target	51
Negotiation Strategy in China	63
Buying Bankrupt Assets	71
Labor Issues in M&A	77
Tax Planning in M&A	87
Converting a Chinese Company into an FIE	93
Common Mistakes	103
Glossary of Terms	107

M&A Environment in China

1 Mergers & Acquisition

Mergers & Acquisitions (M&A) is a general term used to refer to the consolidation of companies. A merger is a combination of two companies to form a new company, while an acquisition is the purchase of one company by another with no new company being formed.

A merger occurs when one firm assumes all the assets and all the liabilities of another. A majority vote of shareholders is generally required to approve a merger. One company can acquire another in several other ways, including purchasing some or all of the company's assets or buying up its outstanding shares of stock.

Introduction

China's economic reforms and robust growth have fuelled an increased pace of M&A activity. The country's World Trade Organization (WTO) accession has opened previously closed industry sectors to foreign investment, and is gradually allowing greater access to its domestic market for Foreign-Invested Enterprises (FIEs).

Inward M&A transactions offering immediate access to a very competitive domestic market are becoming an increasing attractive alternative to green field investments. In addition, outward M&A investments are booming, as many more Chinese companies need, and are able to pursue, opportunities overseas.

Although it used to be more popular for foreign investors to establish FIEs in China from scratch, in recent years there has been an influx of foreign investors using M&A strategies with existing entities. In the current Chinese market there are many benefits of using M&A over establishing new companies. Investors

---

C. Devonshire-Ellis et al. (eds.), *Mergers & Acquisitions in China*, China Briefing,
DOI: 10.1007/978-3-642-14919-1_1, © Asia Briefing Ltd. 2011

are not only able to forgo lengthy set up processes, but are able to analyze the situation, know the existing problems and prepare for the exact market they are about to enter.

Although the number of transactions has significantly increased over the years, average deal sizes are reportedly still under US$20 million, and the few larger transactions always have to undergo a painstakingly long and in-depth approval process. However, it appears that legal factors which may have previously hindered companies from undertaking M&A activity are being addressed by the Chinese government, and as a result the likelihood is that cross-border M&A activity is poised to increase.

The previously incomplete and confusing legal framework surrounding Chinese M&A is rapidly adjusting to the new M&A market. Yet, the Chinese investment law system has conflicting goals; while they would like to protect State-Owned Enterprises (SOEs) from the influx of strong global competitors, they also want to take advantage of the opportunities that western business and technology has to offer. So although the investment rules are becoming clearer, there are still contradictions and legislative gaps.

With the relaxation of many industry-related regulations, increasing sales of SOEs and restructuring of FIEs in China, the opportunities for M&A activities are rapidly increasing, and many foreign companies are taking advantage of the new investment methods. At the same time, it is important for foreign companies looking for M&A opportunities to understand the China market, the process and regulations for M&A in China and, of course, what they are actually buying and for how much.

Concurrently with this market reform, China has been restructuring its state-owned assets. In some sectors, the government is encouraging SOEs to consolidate into large integrated conglomerates, intended to be global leaders in their fields, while in other sectors, the state is seeking to reduce its equity. These new potential targets offer foreign investors new market entry options.

In 2010, China accounted for 36 percent of the US$242.2 billion in deals in the Asia-Pacific region excluding Japan as of July 2, 2010; and had a total of more than US$100 billion in each of the previous three years, according to data compiled by Bloomberg. China-related M&A is not one-way traffic. M&A goes in three directions—outward investment, inward investment, and domestic consolidation. The government's encouragement has been instrumental not only in the surge in M&A overseas but also in promoting domestic consolidation. It is not ready to put "for sale" signs on all its prized assets, however. The Ministry of Commerce (MOFCOM) still treads carefully when it comes to approving certain large scale deals and still offers great protection to domestic industries by shielding them from foreign competition until they grow stronger.

While trying to guard against the possibility that FIEs will come to dominate all the key sectors of the economy, the government has continued to expand the number of industries open to foreign M&A investment. The government has thus cited the importance of M&A activity in this restructuring and privatization process.

In addition, the limitations on investment in many industries are being removed resulting in increased M&A activity. A number of state-owned companies are cleaning up their standards and portfolios and becoming more attractive to foreign investors; at the same time various well-managed private companies are entering this field. Over the past couple of years, some private sector companies (e.g., Alibaba) have captured the attention of investors, but most M&A deals still involve SOEs which typically dominate most sectors. But this is gradually changing and a number of China's private companies are slowly but surely entering the arena. With lower average costs and higher productivity they are beginning to challenge the SOEs in terms of product quality and market share.

However, multinational companies pursuing this path and hoping to tap into China's M&A potential should be aware of the risks and challenges involved. Notably, these companies must be sufficiently equipped on a local level and understand that conventional approaches to M&A cannot be simply applied to the Chinese market. In particular, overseas enterprises cannot maintain the degree of authority or control that they may desire or secure elsewhere in the world. The risk of post-deal failure is also significant. Imagine a scenario where an MNC takes over an SOE and then tries to work together in harmony. Of course, the transition process will be difficult and appeasing the existing staff with new methodology as well as overcoming cultural barriers etc., will be difficult.

Other aspects such as the lack of traditional valuation methods and difficulty in obtaining reliable financial data will also create further hurdles. In short, companies must be willing to devote more time to due diligence.

Getting in Early

China has committed to establishing itself as the manufacturing center of the world. At the same time China's allegiance to WTO will result in an explosion of service industry opportunities across finance, logistics, professional services and other such services over the coming years.

With this rapid opening up of the market and China's desire to establish itself as the world's manufacturing hub, many companies are now realizing that they may have been too slow to react and that it could be too late to invest. However, taking over a well-established existing company can create a number of advantages. For example, you will benefit from a quick build up phase and time to market, as well as minimizing the risk of failure. Furthermore, you can take advantage of existing operating facilities, distribution networks, production knowledge, and intellectual property and existing legal and financial structures etc. As a result, foreign companies are beginning to capitalize on China's lucrative manufacturing base and are realizing that an acquisition is often the cheapest and fastest way to create a low-cost manufacturing base, take advantage of the already existing high quality products and services, and grab market share in China.

Foreign Investment Industrial Guidance Catalog

The PRC law states that companies in China are currently not allowed to engage in "all lawful activities" and must have a clear "business scope," approved by the government authorities, that clearly defines the range of business activities they wish to undertake. The Catalog (updated on October 31, 2007, and effective as of December 1, 2007) groups certain industries and sectors into the following categories—encouraged, restricted and prohibited—and foreign investment projects falling under these areas are subject to scrutiny by the authorities before approval. Projects not included in these categories are considered permitted. Depending on the classification, different levels of approvals are required and in some cases additional approval may be necessary. There may also be restrictions or variations such as on the foreign investor's equity percentage holding of a joint venture. Various industries are still restricted from foreign participation even though the WTO transition period may have expired.

Generally speaking, foreign investors must adopt a special investment vehicle, namely FIEs in the form of Equity Joint Ventures (EJVs), Co-operative Joint Ventures (CJVs) and Wholly Foreign Owned Enterprises (WFOEs). Foreign investors can also set up Representative Offices (ROs). JVs and WFOEs take the form of Limited Liability Companies (LLCs) which do not issue shares but have total investment and registered capital. JVs, WFOEs and FICEs are collectively known as "Foreign-Invested Enterprises" (more information on these various entities can be found in the other China Briefing technical guides).

Different rules apply to different special investment vehicles. For instance, EJVs distribute the company's profits and losses in accordance with each party's proportion of contribution in the registered capital while CJVs are allowed to decide on their profit and capital contribution distribution and time of FDI repatriation within their own parties. WFOEs, on the other hand, have a less clearly laid out organizational structure required by law and thus have more flexibility.

For the purposes of M&A, only FIEs of interest are discussed as follows.

2 Equity Joint Ventures (EJVs) and Contractual Joint Ventures (CJVs)

There are two types of JVs in China, the Equity JV (EJV) and the Co-operative JV (CJV) (sometimes known as the Contractual JV). They may appear similar on the surface but have different implications for the structuring of your entity in China.

An EJV is a joint venture between Chinese and foreign partners where the profits and losses are distributed between the parties in proportion to their respective equity interests in the EJV. The company enjoys limited liability and is a "Chinese legal person."

The CJV is a very flexible FIE where Chinese and foreign investors have more contractual freedom to structure cooperation. It is a joint venture between Chinese and foreign investors where the profits and losses are distributed between the parties in accordance with the specific provisions in the CJV contract, not necessarily in proportion to their respective equity interests in the CJV.

In the past, CJVs took one of two different forms—a "true" CJV which did not involve the creation of a legal person that was separate and distinct from the contracting parties; and a "legal person" CJV in which a separate business entity was established and the parties' liability was generally limited to their capital contributions.

In the case of a "true" CJV, each party was responsible for making its own contributions to the venture, paying its own taxes on profit derived from the venture and bearing its own liability for risks and losses. In contrast, a "legal person" CJV, the more prevalent form today, shares more of the characteristics of an EJV. The "true" CJV is rare today as few investors are willing to entertain the prospect of unlimited liability and so the rest of this discussion only refers to "legal person" CJVs.

In practice, EJVs are more common. There are significant operational differences between the contracts and laws governing the two types. The key differences and practical issues are discussed below.

Liability Status

EJVs must be established as limited liability companies, while CJVs have the option to operate either as a limited liability company or as a non-legal person. Where CJV is set up as a non-legal person, liability is unlimited, but split between the parties in a ratio according to their equity investment.

Management Structure

EJVs must have a two-tier structure, consisting of a board of directors and a contractually appointed manager and/or management team, usually defined as the "general manager and two deputies" (although the precise number of deputies varies), who have legal responsibility for the daily operations of the business. This is to ensure that the specific management functions of a larger operation are clearly defined. CJVs can operate solely as a board of directors (or management committee if non-legal status), but they must have a general manager as well. For smaller concerns, decision-making responsibility can then rest solely with the board.

Contractual Obligations

In real operational terms, EJVs tend to be far more rigid in their contractual structure, thus lending greater security to the larger amounts of equity that such structures are typically used for, albeit that such security is defined more by state regulations. CJVs allow greater contractual flexibility for the investors to define the obligations of the interested parties.

Capital Contributions

Contributions to any JV can be in the form of either cash, or in kind, such as buildings, machinery, materials, and know-how. This process and the value attached to contributions are highly scrutinized. Independent valuers are often used to ensure that "items thus identified are not higher than the prevailing international market prices," as they form an inalienable part of the contractual agreement.

Profit Sharing and Equity Ratios

EJVs are defined contractually as each investor being entitled to profit sharing based upon the proportion of equity owned. CJVs differ fundamentally, in that the profit sharing ratio does not have to be tied to the equity stake. Thus, a foreign partner can own less of the equity than the Chinese partner, but take out more in profit. In some restricted industries the foreign partner must own less, such as advertising, telecoms, real estate and transportation. Profits in CJVs can also be taken "in kind," whereby the Chinese party would undertake processing, with the foreign party realizing profits through the sale of finished goods. This is common in real estate CJVs, where the Chinese side provides land use rights as their equity, and the foreign side provides the finance, and finished units which are then distributed on a contractually agreed ratio as profits.

Reclaiming Capital Investment

CJVs, but not EJVs, can theoretically allow for the original capital injected by the foreign party (but not the Chinese) to be recovered in an accelerated repayment structure during the term of the venture. This is of great assistance when the foreign party is using loan capital to finance the venture. The trade off, however, is that the Chinese side then has title to the CJVs assets after the expiration of the JV term.

However, the State Council did issue a Circular in 2002 to deal with such accelerated repayment structures. This now makes it very difficult to obtain approval for such arrangements.

3 Wholly Foreign-Owned Enterprises (WFOEs)

A WFOE is a company wholly-owned by foreign investors. Note that in general international terminology, if there are several parties jointly investing in a company, this is commonly defined as a Joint Venture. However, according to Chinese Law, when foreign parties are jointly investing in China, without any local partner, the company will always be regarded as a WFOE.

In legal terms, WFOEs are limited liability companies. The liability of the shareholders is limited to the assets they brought to the business.

Foreign-Invested Companies Limited by Shares

It is also possible for foreign investors to establish or buy into companies limited by shares. If companies limited by shares fulfil certain preconditions they can qualify as FIEs. As a result they must be regarded as separate investment vehicles.

Chinese Legislation on M&A

1 Introduction

The Chinese Government enacted provisions in 2003 allowing for the direct acquisition of Chinese limited companies by foreign companies. This applies as much to private companies as it does to SOEs, and includes not only the company, but also its business and assets. This means that overseas investors can merge with Chinese enterprises either by way of stock purchase or asset purchase, and that overseas businesses that merge with domestic enterprises can enjoy preferential taxation treatment. The 2003 provisions specifically addressed the issue of acquiring privately owned Chinese companies and laid down for the first time in a single piece of legislation the relevant principles, procedures and requirements for conducting an equity related acquisition.

On August 8, 2006, MOFCOM, the State-Owned Assets Supervision and Administration Commission (SASAC) and four other government agencies issued the *Rules on Merger with and Acquisition of Domestic Enterprises by Foreign Investors* (Order No. 10, 2006 Rules), which was subsequently amended in June 2009. These rules provide clarification of the provisional rules issued in 2003 and further regulate M&A requirements and procedures. The aim of this legislation is to ensure standard treatment for acquisitions while protecting "national economic security".

The 2006 Rules only cover the acquisition of equity interest in domestic limited liability companies and companies limited by shares established according to the PRC Company Law. In contrast, there are no limitations as to the nature of the foreign investor, who could consequently be a company, an individual or any other business entity.

As the 2006 Rules apply only to the merger and acquisition of domestic firms, foreign investors seeking to acquire firms in China that already enjoy FIE status must adhere to a different set of regulations. The *Several Provisions on Changes in Equity Interest of Investors in Foreign-Invested Enterprises* (published by the

C. Devonshire-Ellis et al. (eds.), *Mergers & Acquisitions in China*, China Briefing, DOI: 10.1007/978-3-642-14919-1_2, © Asia Briefing Ltd. 2011

Ministry of Foreign Trade and Economic Cooperation on May 28, 1997) governs matters concerning the reporting and approval of all changes in the equity structure of an FIE. Matters not addressed by these provisions shall be handled "with reference" to the 2006 Rules.

Before taking a closer look at the provisions of the 2006 Rules, it is useful to be reminded that M&A deals in China can have different forms. For each specific form, a specific provision applies. Therefore, it is very important to evaluate at the initial stage under which form the deal you are conducting, or think to conduct, falls. The main forms are the following: (a) acquisitions or mergers of privately-owned enterprises; (b) acquisitions or mergers of foreign-invested enterprises (WFOEs or JVs); (c) acquisitions of state-owned enterprises; (d) acquisitions of listed companies.

Major Objectives of the Rules

- To consolidate the existing rules governing foreign M&A activities in China
- To set out clear requirements and procedures regarding the acquisition of equity interests and assets of domestic enterprises by foreign investors
- To introduce anti-trust provisions in respect of such acquisitions
- To standardize the acquisition procedure
- To protect national security

2 Regulatory Issues for Acquiring Privately-Held (Domestic) Companies

Below are some of the major regulatory issues that must be considered when a foreign investor is to conduct M&A transactions with domestic enterprises in China. Issues to be discussed include the transformation of a domestic enterprise to a foreign-invested enterprise and the resulting requirements to comply with FIE rules, the derivation of transaction price, the equity purchase agreement, the approval and registration processes, issues of payment, and anti-monopoly considerations.

Compliance with FIE Rules

Foreign investors that acquire a privately held company will need to convert it to a Foreign Invested Enterprise. As a result, all related FIE rules and regulations must be observed. These include restrictions relating to the available investment

2 Regulatory Issues for Acquiring Privately-Held (Domestic) Companies

vehicle, the necessary qualifications of investors, the possible scope of business, and the minimum registered capital.

Restrictions on Types of M&A

According to article 4 of the 2006 Rules, mergers or acquisitions may not result in:

1. Foreign investors' creation of a WFOE in the acquired enterprise in industries where no WFOE is allowed under the *Catalog on the Guidance of Foreign Investment Industries*
2. Foreign investors becoming a controlling party or relatively controlling party in an acquired enterprise in industries which require the Chinese party to be controlling or relatively controlling
3. Foreign investors acquiring any enterprise engaged in industries where operation by foreign investors is prohibited

Furthermore, MOFCOM approval is required for deals involving "key industries", affecting or possibly affecting "national economic security" or resulting in the transfer of the actual right of control over a domestic enterprise that owns any "well-known trademark or China's time-honored brands". The wording here is ambiguous. It is unclear as to what a "key industry" is, what will affect "economic security", and exactly what constitutes a "well-known trademark". Additionally, it is unclear what steps must be taken in order to gain approval for acquiring one of the above such domestic enterprises.

Registered Capital

After a foreign investor purchases the equity rights of a domestic company, and the domestic company has been changed to an FIE, the FIE's registered capital shall be the registered capital of the original domestic enterprise, and the investment contribution by the foreign investor shall be the proportion of the purchased equity in the original registered capital.

Additionally, when a foreign investor merges with a domestic enterprise by equity merger, article 19 of the 2006 Rules places upper limits on the total investment amount of the foreign-funded enterprise established after the merger. The upper limit on investment is determined by the total amount of registered capital as outlined in the table below.

Registered capital	Upper limit on investment
US$2.1 million or below	10/7 of registered capital
Above US$2.1 and up to US$5 million	2 times registered capital
Above US$5 and up to US$12	2.5 times registered capital
Above US$12 million	3 times registered capital

Previous regulations laid down a minimum foreign investment of 25% in the equity of a Sino-foreign joint venture, but did not address the permissibility or handling of smaller investments, which were dealt with locally on an ad hoc basis.

Article 9 of the 2006 Rules provides that, where the ratio of a foreign investors' capital contribution to the registered capital of an FIE established as a result of M&A is less than 25 percent, the enterprise shall not be entitled to the treatment for FIEs.

Transaction Price

All M&As between a foreign and domestic enterprise should determine the transaction price on the basis of the result of an evaluation conducted by an asset evaluation institution. The parties may choose the asset evaluation institution themselves, but it must be established within the territory of China in accordance with the law.

The Ministry of Finance (MOF) released the *Measures for the Administration of the Examination and Approval of Asset Appraisal Institutions*, effective June 1, 2005. These measures were intended to standardize the asset appraisal industry to a degree as the requirements and process of establishing an asset appraisal institution are formalized and implemented.

Article 14 of the 2006 Rules further prohibit the transfer of equity interest or sale of assets at a price "obviously lower" than the evaluation result for the purpose of transferring the capital out of China in a disguised way. However, this clause is vague and there is no clear definition of the "price".

Equity Purchase Agreement

The foreign investor and domestic enterprise are to conclude an equity purchase agreement, or in the case of foreign investors' subscription to the capital increase of the target, a capital increase agreement. Article 22 of the 2006 Rules provide that the agreement should contain the following:

1. The relevant information of the parties in the agreement
2. The amount of equity to be purchased or capital to be increased, and the price to be paid
3. The term and method of performance of the agreement
4. The rights and obligations of each party
5. The liabilities for breach of agreement and the means by which disputes will be settled
6. The date and place of the conclusion of the agreement

Verification

The establishment of FIEs as well as changes in FIE-investors and equity require verification by the National Development and Reform Commission (NDRC); but only in the case of big projects, i.e., encouraged and permitted industry projects, with a total investment of US$100 million and restricted industry projects with a total investment of US$50 million. Verification serves as a check on the project in relation to the following issues:

1. Compliance with FIE laws and regulations
2. Compliance with requirements of the medium to long-term plans for the development of the national economy and society, the industry plan and the policy for the adjustment of the industrial structure
3. Compliance with the public interest and relevant state anti-monopoly provisions
4. Compliance with land use plans, the urban master plan and environmental protection policies
5. Compliance with the technical and process standards prescribed by the state
6. Compliance with relevant state provisions on administration of the capital account and control of foreign debts

While regulations stipulate that verification is required prior to commencement of approval, in practice the two are often conducted simultaneously.

Some points to note:

- provincial government authorities may approve foreign investment projects of US$100 million in the "encouraged" or "permitted" foreign investment categories and US$50 million for projects in the "restricted" foreign investment category
- the NDRC must approve categories with a larger investment, and the State Council must approve projects with an investment of more than US$500 million in the "encouraged" or "permitted" categories and projects more than US$100 million in the "restricted" category

The verification authority is to be presented with the following information:

1. The project term, the term of operation and basic details regarding the investor(s)
2. The scale of the project, the main establishment particulars and products, the principal technologies and processes to be used, the target markets(s) for the products and the planned workforce
3. The location of the project, requirements concerning such resources as land, water energy etc., and consumption of principal raw materials
4. An environmental impact assessment
5. The pricing when public products and services are involved

6. The total investment of the project, its registered capital, the respective capital contributions of the parties, the methods of contribution, the financing plan and the equipment that needs to be imported, including related costs

The application must be accompanied by the following documents:

1. The Chinese and foreign investors' enterprise registration certificates (business licenses), commercial registration certificates, the most recently audited financial statements (including balance sheet, profit and loss statement and cash flow statement) and documentary proof of the parties' creditworthiness
2. An investment proposal and a board resolution concerning the acquisition
3. A letter of intent regarding the financing issued by a financial institution
4. An opinion regarding the environmental impact assessment from the provincial level or the state administrative department in charge of environmental protection
5. An opinion on the zoning of the selected site issued by the provincial-level planning department
6. An opinion on the preliminary examination of the potential site of the project issued by the provincial-level or state land resources department
7. If capital contributions are made in the form of state-owned assets or land use rights, the confirmation document issued by the competent department

The NDRC must issue a decision on a project within 20 days of its receipt of the application, but may extend its decision deadline another 10 days upon notice to the applicant. The NDRC can outsource a project review to a consultant, which postpones the start of the 20 day clock, but the decision on retaining a consultant must be made within 5 days of application receipt.

Approval Process

Government approval is required for transactions involving:
Encouraged or permitted projects:

- total investment over US$100 million—require approval of MOFCOM and NDRC
- under US$100 million—approval from provincial- or lower-level ministries

  Restricted projects:

- exceeding US$50 million—national-level approval from the MOFCOM and NDRC
- less than US$50 million—approval from provincial-level offices of the Ministries

Approval of other specialized administrative agencies may be required in certain industries.

2 Regulatory Issues for Acquiring Privately-Held (Domestic) Companies

The investor is required to submit the following documents:

1. If the domestic enterprise is a limited liability company, the resolution of the shareholders on unanimous consent of the foreign investor's equity merger. If the domestic company is a stock limited company, the resolution of the shareholders meeting on consent of the foreign investor's equity merger
2. The application for the domestic company to be converted to an FIE
3. The contract and articles of association of the FIE to be established
4. The agreement regarding the assignment of equity interest or the subscription to the increased equity interest
5. The financial audit report of the domestic company from the previous year
6. The investor's identification certification or incorporation certification and credit certification, to be notarized and legally attested
7. A statement concerning the enterprises that the domestic enterprise has invested in
8. The business licenses of the domestic company, in duplicate, and the business licenses of the enterprises it has invested in, in duplicate
9. The plan for re-settlement of the domestic enterprise's employees
10. The agreement on the disposition of the claims and debts of the domestic enterprise, should such an agreement be reached between the foreign investor and the local enterprise
11. The result from the asset evaluation conducted by a proper asset evaluation institution
12. A statement disclosing whether or not the two parties are affiliated. Should both parties be under the control of the same third party, a disclosure of the identity of the third party, an explanation of the purpose of the acquisition, and evidence that the result of the asset evaluation reflects fair market value
13. If the acquisition triggers the reporting requirements under applicable anti-trust rules, the respective supporting documents
14. Relevant permission documents if the scope or scale of business or the acquisition of land use rights of the newly established FIE requires permission from the other authorities

The MOFCOM will announce its acceptance or rejection of the application within 30 days of receipt of the necessary documents. In the case that the MOFCOM accepts the application, it will present a certificate of approval.

Registration Process

Upon receipt of the approval certificate from the MOFCOM, the foreign enterprise has 30 days to register the acquired domestic enterprise as an FIE with the SAIC or its local subbranches. The merged domestic company is responsible for applying for a modification of its registration with the original registration administrative authority and for obtaining a foreign investment enterprise's business license.

When applying for modification of registration, the merged domestic company shall supply the following documents:

1. The application for modification of the registration
2. The agreement on the foreign investor's purchase of the shareholders' equity of the domestic company or on the subscription of the domestic company to increase capital
3. The amended articles of association of the company or the amendment to the original articles of association, and if applicable, the joint venture contract if the company is not converted into a WFOE
4. The approval certificate of the FIE
5. The foreign investor's identification documents or certificate of commencement of business
6. The amended name list of the board of directors, documents stating names and residences of newly installed directors, and documents outlining the positions of the new directors
7. Other documents as requested by the SAIC

Within 30 days of the receipt of the FIE business license, the foreign investor shall register with the departments of taxation, customs, land administration, foreign exchange control, etc.

Payment

Timing

The foreign investor shall pay the full amount stated in the Equity Purchase Agreement within 3 months of the receipt of the FIE business license. Under special circumstances and subject to the approval of MOFTEC or the provincial examination and approval authority, the foreign investor can pay a minimum of 60% of the price within 6 months, with the full balance to be paid within 1 year of the issuance of the FIE business license.

If the foreign investor conducts the acquisition through subscription to the capital increase of a domestic enterprise, the foreign investor shall pay no less than 20% of the amount of registered capital to be increased at the time of application for FIE business license. The time limit for payment of remaining increased registered capital is subject to the provisions of Company Law of the People's Republic of China, FIE laws and regulations, and regulations on the registration of companies.

Share Swaps

Share swaps are a new alternative to cash as a financing option for foreign investors engaging in M&A of domestic enterprises. Foreign companies may also

2 Regulatory Issues for Acquiring Privately-Held (Domestic) Companies

pay with a combination of stock and cash. Consideration can be paid in foreign currency, property, intellectual property, and with approval of the State Administration of Foreign Exchange (SAFE), in RMB.

Below are some of the prerequisites that must be met in order to utilize share swaps to finance foreign M&A of domestic enterprises:

1. The foreign company whose shares are to be swapped shall be:
   i. legally established
   ii. in a location that has a sound legal system on company administration
   iii. free from punishment by relevant regulatory authority in the three years prior to the swap
2. The equity from both the domestic company and foreign company shall be legally owned by the shareholders involved and transferable in accordance with applicable law
3. The equity shall be free from any dispute over ownership and not subject to charges or other restrictions
4. The equity of the foreign company shall be listed and traded on an overseas open and lawful securities exchange market
5. The trading price of stocks of the foreign company shall have been stable for the previous year

In the case of M&A via share swaps, the domestic enterprise is required to utilize a merger consultant charged with the duty of conducting due diligence on the authenticity of application documents in the acquisition, the financial status of the foreign company, and whether the acquisition is in compliance with relevant articles in the 2006 Rules. The merger consultant is required to be in good financial and legal standing and possess the capability to perform the above listed duties.

This due diligence requirement is aimed to prevent overseas shell special purpose vehicles (SPVs) from acquiring Chinese assets and to avoid Chinese assets being sold below market value.

Share swap financed M&A are subject to the approval of the MOFCOM which will take around 30 days. On approval, a conditional approval certificate (valid for 6 months) will be issued to the domestic investor. An unconditional approval certificate will only be issued providing all necessary verification and registration procedures are carried out during this sixth month period.

Anti-monopoly Provisions

Foreign mergers and acquisitions of domestic companies or foreign capital investing in domestic companies' operation in other forms should be examined in accordance with relevant laws and regulations if the cases are related to national security.

The 2006 Rules outline a set of situations under which foreign investors acquiring domestic enterprises must report to MOFCOM and SAIC. They are as follows:

1. Either party to the acquisition has a turnover of more than RMB1.5 billion in the Chinese market in the current year
2. The foreign investor has acquired more than ten enterprises engaged in related industries within 1 year
3. The market share of either party exceeds 20% of the Chinese market
4. The acquisition leads to the Chinese market share of any of the parties to exceed 25%

Even in the absence of the above listed conditions, if MOFCOM or SAIC considers the foreign investor will acquire a significant market share as a result of the acquisition, or there are other important factors which may cause a significant effect on competition, the national economy and people's livelihood, or the State's economic security, MOFCOM or SAIC may require a report. Additionally, they may require a report at the request of domestic competitors or the relevant functional authority or trade association.

China's anti-monopoly law has a mandatory security inspection provision on any mergers and acquisitions by foreign investors that may have an impact on state security. The foreign investor must go through a state security inspection before they are allowed to proceed with the merger or acquisition.

The law aims to protect market competition by regulating price-fixing and other forms of collusion, and providing for investigation and prosecution of such practices. The regulative review will consider a company's market share and market power, market structure and concentration, effect on consumers and other relevant business operators, as well as the effect on the development of the national economy and public interest. The new law bans monopolistic agreements, such as price-fixing and other forms of collusion, and provides for investigation and prosecution of monopolistic practices. Its aim is to protect fair competition by prohibiting three kinds of monopoly acts: reaching monopolizing agreements; abusing a dominant market position; and concentration of business operations which may exclude or restrict competition. Conduct subject to an anti-monopoly inspection includes mergers and acquisitions, JVs, as well as licensing and technology transfer.

The anti-monopoly law also prohibits agreements between competitors to fix, maintain or change prices, allocate markets, limit output or sales, or restrict the acquisition or development of new technology. Western observers have raised concerns about some provisions that could be enforced in a discriminatory fashion against foreign companies in China.

Conclusion

A comprehensive legal framework for the process by which foreign investors can acquire purely domestic private firms is gradually evolving. Issues such as the purchase price, the purchase agreements, the approval and registration processes, and payment issues, including a new introduction of share swaps as a means to finance M&A, and the new anti-monopoly legislation continue to be improved.

However, the current M&A regulatory environment in China is far from comprehensive; the new regulations lack full details and will require supplemental legislation and proper interpretation in order to make them effective. It is necessary that foreign investors strive to understand relevant laws and regulations as best as possible, and always lookout for loopholes that arise from insufficient or contradictory clauses.

3 Regulatory Issues Regarding Acquisition of Foreign-invested Enterprises

As mentioned above, the *Several Provisions on Changes in Equity Interest of Investors in Foreign-Invested Enterprises* covers the change of ownership interest of the investors in FIEs in China. The Several Provisions specifically require reporting and approval under the following circumstances of FIE equity restructuring:

- transfer of FIE equity interests among FIE investors
- transfer of equity interest in the FIE to its affiliated company or other transferees
- adjustment, i.e., increase or decrease, in the registered capital of an FIE, leading to changes in its equity structure
- transfer of FIE equity interest to a pledge or any other beneficiary as a result of the use of FIE equity interest as security by one of the investors with the consent of the others
- transfer of equity interest in an FIE due to inheritance, bankruptcy or dissolution
- acquisition of equity interest in an FIE through a merger or spin-off
- change in an investor or in the equity of an investor due to the failure of the investor to make its subscribed capital contributions to the FIE

Compliance with FIE Rules

The provisions also require FIE rules to be observed especially in relation to the availability of particular investment vehicles, e.g., in certain industries, the qualification of respective investors, the maximum foreign equity interest ratio and the minimum registered capital.

When the restructuring of the FIE equity results in the creation of a WFOE from a EJV or CJV, the enterprise shall be subject to the rules and regulations regarding the establishment of a WFOE as stipulated in the *Detailed Rules for the Implementation of the Law of the People's Republic of China on Wholly Foreign-Invested*

Enterprises. Foreign investors shall not be permitted to gain sole ownership of enterprises in industries where sole foreign ownership is prohibited.

Article 5 of the Several Provisions provide that a transfer of FIE equity interest may not result in a situation where the percentage of investment by the foreign investor is less than 25 percent of the registered capital of the FIE (except for in the instance where a foreign investor assigns its entire equity interest to their Chinese joint venture partner).

Transaction Price

It has been standard practice that the parties involved in a transaction of FIE equity are free to arrive at a transaction price themselves, with no regulations or requirements. Meanwhile, the Several Provisions stipulate that if the Chinese investor has invested in state-owned assets, then an outside asset appraisal agency required to appraise the value of the equity interest being transferred.

However, this clause about transaction price is unclear and it would be wise to check this with the competent examination and approval authority.

Ownership Interest Transfer Agreement

Parties involved in the transaction shall enter into an ownership interest transfer agreement which includes the following:

1. Names, addresses, and legal representatives of the assignor and assignee, along with the names, titles, and nationalities of their legal representatives
2. Share and price of the equity to be transferred
3. Time frame and form of the equity transfer
4. The rights and obligations of the assignee pursuant to the articles of association of the FIE
5. Liabilities for breach of contract
6. Governing law and mechanism for settlement of disputes
7. Effective date and termination of the agreement
8. Date and place of conclusion of the agreement

Verification

Verification is required from the NDRC or its sub-branches in the case of changes in FIE-investors and FIE-equity (but only in the case of big projects, i.e., encouraged and permitted industry projects, with a total investment of US$100 million, and restricted industry projects with a total investment of US$50 million). Details discussed in the previous section titled "Regulatory issues concerning acquisition of privately-held companies" apply to the transfer of equity of FIEs as well.

Approval

The transfer of equity interests is also subject to the approval of the responsible examination and approval authority. Unless the changes result in the total amount of investment of the FIE exceeding the scope of its approving authority, the changes should be examined and approved by the examination and approval authority which originally approved the establishment of the FIE. Otherwise the changes may be subject to approval by the examination and approval authority of a higher level.

The following documents are generally required:

1. Application for change of equity interest
2. An executed Equity Interest Transfer Agreement
3. The original Joint Venture Contract and/or Articles of Association of the FIE, and amendments to the Joint Venture Contract and/or Articles of Association, reflecting the changes to the equity structure of the FIE
4. Copies of the original Certificate of Approval and the Business License of the FIE
5. A Board Resolution authorizing the change
6. A list of names of the board members after the transfer of FIE equity interest
7. Written consents of other investors, if transferring to a third party or affiliate
8. Other documents as may be required by the examination and approval authority

The responsible examination and approval authority is to make its decision within 30 days of receiving a complete set of the required documents. The foreign investor shall, within 30 days of receipt of approval from the examination and approval authority, apply for an amendment to its Certificate of Approval of the Foreign-invested Enterprise.

The Chinese investor can apply for cancellation of the Certificate of Approval of Foreign Invested Enterprise within 30 days of approval by the examination and approval authority in the case that he has acquired ownership interest in the enterprise and the FIE will be converted to a domestic enterprise. The examination and approval authority will then send a notice to the original registration authority of the FIE regarding the cancellation of the Certificate of Approval of the Foreign-invested Enterprise.

Registration

The FIE needs to be re-registered within 30 days of the issuance of the new Certificate of Approval. This means the newly structured FIE should file an application with the appropriate office of the SAIC for the registration of the change to equity interests. For this the FIE is required to submit the same set of documents that is submitted to the examination and approval authority, together with the Certificate of Approval and any other documents required by the responsible SAIC.

SAIC will then issue a new Business License to the FIE. Failure to file a registration of the change as required may cause SAIC to issue sanctions such as fines or suspension of the FIE's business license.

Anti-monopoly Provisions

The same rules should also apply here as above with the equity transfer of private enterprises.

Conclusion

The most important thing to realize is that the transfer of equity interests in FIEs, even between two foreign investors, requires state verification and approval. One ambiguity in this area is whether or not transactions involving the transfer of equity interests in FIEs would require an outside asset appraisal organ to perform an asset valuation, as required in the case of an acquisition of a purely domestic private firm or SOE. Consultation with the appropriate authorities is recommended.

4 Regulatory Issues for Acquiring State-owned Companies

State holding corporations are unable to effectively exercise ownership functions, as they are prone to interference from government agencies, and often lack the capacity to monitor and control management behavior within their corporate structure. The door is now wide open for foreign investors to purchase SOEs. China announced significant laws allowing foreigners to buy out China's SOEs with much fewer restrictions than ever. The aim of the law is to utilize foreign capital to rejuvenate China's SOEs.

What is now being encountered is that different legislation and regulations are being introduced by various governmental bodies in order to address the needs of SOEs, however there seems to be little consultancy between any of them. As such, there is constant confusion due to overlapping legislation and general inconsistency. In the specific instance of SOEs that are yet to be converted into a company limited by shares, the basic legal framework seems vague and incomplete. In many cases problems encountered by those looking to make SOE acquisitions can only be overcome by discussions with the relative authorities involved, as requirements are often determined on a case-by-case basis.

Qualification of Foreign Investors

The relevant provisions for foreign investor qualifications are extremely vague and broad. It is possible that this has been done so as to allow authorities to take an interpretative stance on deals involving foreign investors, and allow them the leverage to reject any deal they may deem to be unsatisfactory or simply unwanted. According to the provisions, foreign investors who invest in SOEs or acquire state-owned equity interests shall:

- have the business qualifications and technical ability as required for the operation of the target
- have a good business reputation and management capabilities
- have a solid financial position and economic strengths

Offshore structures such as special purpose vehicles established outside China for the purpose of holding FIE equity onshore may become quite vulnerable under these provisions as they are often established with minimal investment.

Reorganization and Owners Consent

Chinese law states that the "competent department in charge of foreign trade and economic cooperation" requires foreign investors to submit a reorganization plan before initiating the approval process.

Consent must also be obtained by the target company from its owner, this being the government department in charge of the document, the business holding the state-owned equity interest or any respective investor that has been given authority by the state.

Appraisal

Special appraisal procedures have been introduced in order to prevent the below-market-price sale of state-owned property rights. Regulations state that an appraisal of the acquisition object, be it property rights of a target SOE or state-owned equity interests or assets, must be conducted by a competent state-owned appraisal authority. It is this appraisal that will eventually determine the price of the acquisition.

Sale and Purchase of Property Rights

Transferring state-owned property rights can be done by auction, bidding or agreements. The owner of the targeted state-owned property rights must publish (via a property rights transaction institution) the details of the proposed transaction, which doubles as an invitation for other potential transferees. In the case of two or more investors indicating interest, the transfer is decided by way of bidding or an auction, although this is not very common.

Generally there is only one interested party, in which case the transfer is conducted by way of agreement. Regulations stipulate that this agreement should contain:

- name and address of both transferor and transferee
- details of the state-owned property right(s) to be transferred
- settlement arrangements for staff and workers
- arrangements regarding claims and debts of the target
- details of the price, payment method and conditions of payment
- the sharing of tax obligations regarding the transfer
- the dispute settlement mechanism
- any liabilities for contract breach
- conditions for any amendments and/or termination of the contract
- any other terms considered necessary by the involved parties

Approval and Verification

Stipulations involving the acquisition of property rights in SOEs are unclear at best. Again confusion reigns here because the role and interactions between different responsible bodies and regimes is not clearly defined. In terms of state-owned shares, foreign investors may also purchase shares in previously state-owned targets, provided they qualify as strategic investors. This is subject to SASAC approval. The following documents need to be submitted to SASAC in order for the approval process to begin:

- resolution regarding state-owned assets, this includes submitting a feasibility study, financial details of the party from the last 3 years, reorganization plan and staff settlement documents
- a basic program containing information on the transfer
- the state-owned property right registration certificate of both the target company and the investor
- a legal opinion submitted by a law firm
- details of the transferee
- other details stipulated by SASAC

Once the approval process has been completed, the newly established FIE will need to be registered with the competent authority. If there is to be capital contributions made to the transfer in the form of land use rights, a confirmation document from the relevant authority must be submitted to the NDRC for verification.

Mechanism for Purchase

Foreign investors can purchase Chinese SOEs through three venues: the local assets and equity exchange, the match-making of the intermediaries, and through the framework of the state holding corporations. (More information on this can be found in Chap. 6.)

5 Regulatory Issues for Acquiring Listed Companies

Unlike many of the companies in China, including FIEs, which make up the majority of the business in the country, companies limited by shares require a complex corporate structure. However, they also allow the company much easier access to public funding.

These Chinese businesses can be FIEs, and the practice of tax authorities seems to indicate that the FIE tax benefits in China would also apply to foreign-invested companies limited by shares. However, there are some legal requirements for FIEs limited by shares to be legally recognized in China:

- total capital is constituted by shares of equal par value
- shareholders undertake liability in accordance with the shares they subscribe for
- the company undertakes liability with all its assets
- Chinese and foreign shareholders hold shares in the company
- the minimum registered capital requirement for a FIE limited by shares is RMB5 million. A listed company is a type of company limited by shares

China's capital markets are still comparatively immature compared to those overseas, and acquisition by means of share purchase, while growing, is still in the minority. The regulations and statutes governing the listed companies, including the transfers of both shares and assets has been in a constant state of development and evolution. Needless to say, this has generated a large inconsistency among governing authorities.

Listed Shares

Chinese law makes a legal distinction between listed and unlisted shares, of which listed shares are divided into three categories, namely A-shares, B-shares and shares listed overseas.

A-shares are traditionally reserved for Chinese businesses or individuals, however foreign investors may purchase up to 10% of A-shares in a Chinese listed company provided they qualify as a Qualified Institutional Investor (QFII). But note that preconditions for this status are tough. In order for the China Securities Regulatory Commission (CSRC) to approve a QFII application, the foreign investor must be one of the following:

- a fund management institution with operational experience of no less than 5 years and with managed assets of at least US$5 billion in the last financial year
- an insurance company also with 5 years of operational experience and security assets of US$5 billion from the last financial year
- a securities house with at least 30 years of operational experience and managed security assets of a minimum of US$10 billion in the last financial year
- a commercial bank with a minimum US$10 billion in managed security assets in the last financial year, and a rating among the top 100 in the world (in terms of total assets)
- other institutional investors which have been established for at least 5 years and have either managed or held securities of US$5 billion or more in the last financial year

B-shares are RMB-denominated shares and can only be purchased and traded for in foreign currency and are traditionally reserved for foreign entities or individuals. However the number of B-shares compared to A-shares in a listed company is quite small, and in most cases, companies have not issued B-shares at all.

Unlisted Shares

In the past, implementing acquisition or merger strategies by way of listed share purchase was totally inappropriate due to the high restrictions placed on foreign investors. Because of this, investors wishing to purchase listed companies did so by buying unlisted shares. This prompted a ban on foreign purchase of unlisted shares in 1995. When the ban was lifted in 2002, it was done so with the provision of tight restrictions placed on foreign investments in this area

The unlisted shares can be purchased by either an agreement between the purchaser and the target shareholders or by a tender offer. A tender offer involves the purchaser acquiring the shares of the target according to the terms of a public statement to the target shareholders. This offer is subject to strict CSRC verification, and is only possible provided there is full payment in cash or stock.

General Offer

In addition, the CSRC has promulgated the new *Measures on Takeover of Listed Companies*. They introduce a more flexible tender offer system and a new disclosure requirement:

- new tender offer system—investors taking control of more than 30% of a listed company will no longer be required to offer to buy all of its outstanding shares. The old rule thwarted many potential acquisitions of listed companies.
- disclosure requirements—investors taking control of 5% of a listed company must make a public announcement; and if an investor holds over 20% it should make a detailed disclosure of its financial status.

If a foreign investor, without QFII status, purchases a controlling stock of unlisted shares in a target, this would require a waiver of the public offer requirement from the CSRC. Generally speaking, the CSRC has looked favorably at these waiver applications as it is considered to be beneficial to the Chinese economy. This waiver can be granted in the following situations:

- there is de facto no change in control over the listed company
- the listed target company is in financial trouble and the investor intends to save and restructure the target with the consent of its shareholders. This is also subject to a lock-up period of 3 years
- the target company issues new shares leading to the investor purchasing and owning at least 30% of the issued shares. This is also subject to the target's shareholders consenting to the waiver of the general offer requirement.

A Backlash Against Foreign Investments in China?

These measures were not welcomed in all quarters and some companies have accused China of becoming protectionist. However, we believe in fact that that these rules will actually foster deal activity. For example, the new share swap system creates more room for the growth of domestic companies, and will encourage multinationals to use M&A.

Equally, the more flexible tender offer system will provide the acquiring company with more options, while reducing costs and increasing takeover efficiency. The new disclosure requirements, which increases the acquirer's transparency, will protect the interests of small investors, and the anti-trust review will provide better investigation into foreign monopolies, blocking deals that might hurt economic security and consumer interests.

This improved legislation is in line with China's transition into a market economy. Every developed economy has anti-trust legislations—monopolies can act against the public interest—so why should not China? In a fully open economy, there are very few legal differences between a foreign and a domestic firm, besides some national security controls. We think it is more reasonable to see all these measures as a sign of the increasing maturity of the Chinese system—and we should welcome them.

Structuring Your Own Merger and Acquisition

Ensuring an M&A deal is completed effectively and efficiently requires strict adherence to certain processes and the carrying out of extensive due diligence. Foreign companies must have clear objectives as to what kind of structure they require and at the same time understand what they are trying to achieve through an M&A transaction, as this will greatly affect their choice of target industry, market segmentation, geography, corporate structure, operating objectives, taxation implications and business scope.

In China, the high tax rates and non-transparent regulations often mean that many FIEs consider conducting transactions "offshore" when acquiring assets. A relatively high number of FIEs in China use a holding company, based in Hong Kong or elsewhere that offer more transparent tax jurisdictions and more flexibility as well as efficiency when transferring interests. In this way, to make an investment in China, a second offshore company can simply purchase the shares of the first company under the laws of the jurisdiction in question. The Chinese government is thus not permitted to regulate such actions and no approval is needed.

Traditionally, foreign investors have sought to create a new FIE in order to implement their Chinese investment projects. These FIEs have been established in the form of Joint Ventures (JVs) or Wholly Foreign-Owned Enterprises (WFOEs), with WFOEs being the preferred option, as investing companies can gain complete control of their investment interests.

1 Type of Activity

Setting up an FIE in China has its advantages in that the project can be shaped and controlled to the investors needs. Local authorities in China are also familiar with this type of deal structure. An M&A transaction in China may be consummated through one of the following ways:

C. Devonshire-Ellis et al. (eds.), *Mergers & Acquisitions in China*, China Briefing, DOI: 10.1007/978-3-642-14919-1_3, © Asia Briefing Ltd. 2011

- equity acquisition;
- asset acquisition;
- merger;
- off-shore equity acquisition.

Of which the most common is an equity purchase or an asset acquisition. A merger or off-shore equity acquisition may take place but are decidedly rarer.

Due to the restrictions placed on foreign businesses' activities in China, foreign investors have steered away from direct investment, and have looked to invest through holding companies set up outside of China with the specific purpose of holding the equity interest in an onshore FIE. These holding companies are often referred to as special purpose vehicles.

Equity acquisition—acquisition of equity interests or shares in PRC domestic companies by foreign companies:

- acquisition of equity interests or shares from existing investors of a PRC domestic company; and/or
- subscription of newly increased registered capital or new shares in such a company.

An equity transaction is subject to full approval of the Chinese authorities and thus is time-consuming and may also expose you to existing liabilities. An investor will assume all of the existing obligations, liabilities and restrictions of the target company so careful due diligence must be carried out. Despite the greater risks from inherited liabilities, equity acquisitions tend to still be more popular in China compared to asset acquisitions, mainly due to the higher taxes associated with asset deals.

Asset acquisition—acquisition of assets of domestic enterprises by foreign investors:

- foreign investor setting up a new FIE in China and using the new FIE to acquire assets from a PRC domestic enterprise and to operate such assets; or
- foreign investor acquiring assets from a PRC domestic enterprise and using such assets as its capital contribution to form a new FIE, including WFOEs.

In the past, acquisitions by foreign investors of assets from PRC domestic enterprises and the use of such assets as their contributions to newly established FIEs were not common practice.

The preferred acquisition method will also depend on various considerations such as the financial conditions of the target, the required governmental approvals, the transaction time, and the tax consequences of the structure, and as such would require thorough due diligence.

Here is a comparison of equity vs. asset acquisition:

Type of acquisition	Advantages	Disadvantages
Equity-related acquisition	Less administration issues—requires government approval and registration but no other transfer procedures	Subject to full approval of the Chinese authorities; time-consuming and may expose you to existing liabilities (i.e. social welfare)
	Less fuss than an asset deal with respect to taxes	Existing partners have the right to veto the transaction
	Operational licenses should be already in place	Investor will assume all of the existing obligations, liabilities and restrictions of the target company
		May require more extensive due diligence and pre-planning
Asset-related acquisition	Investor may choose the preferred assets of the target company	More complex and involves different procedural requirements for the transfer of different assets and liabilities of the target company
	Any existing obligations, liabilities or restrictions will remain the responsibility of the target company	Establishment of a new FIE will require separate approval from the authorities and operational licenses
	If new FIEs are established some preferential policies may be available	Tax issues to consider relating to transfer of assets
		Potential severance payments to transferred employees

2 Mergers

By international standards, mergers and acquisitions are generally only distinguished from each other by the terms of how they are marketed. Under Chinese law mergers are only possible as onshore transactions. Therefore foreign investors must have set up a FIE in China in order to be able to complete a merger deal. There are two types of mergers:

Mergers by "absorption"—the absorption of one company by another whereby one company is dissolved and its registered capital and assets are merged into the remaining entity. The legal entity of the absorbed business would then cease to exist.

Merger by new establishment—each of the companies in question are dissolved and a new legal entity is formed by combining the assets and registered capital of the old companies.

3 Offshore Acquisition

In this scenario an investor may purchase some or all of the off-shore shares held by the company's foreign parent(s) thus acquiring or increasing control of the target company. This option is only possible in the case that the target company has a foreign parent and it would only apply to the acquisition of the foreign investors' equity.

Acquisition

1 The Acquisition Procedure

Initial Steps: Letters of Intent

Usually, the Chinese party will approach the foreign investor or potential investor with a draft "letter of intent" or "memorandum of understanding" outlining the fact that the two parties are going to discuss the matter and laying out the complete procedures for doing so up to the actual share transfer.

Once you have chosen your structure, the acquisition will require approval from MOFCOM and registration through the SAIC and its local branches (AICs).

Approval Process for Establishing an FIE

Chinese laws permit foreign investment enterprises in the forms of WFOEs, EJVs, CJVs, and FICEs.

This process requires approval from the Ministry of Commerce (MOFCOM) or its local branch.

The general rules for establishing an FIE are as follows:

Total investment	Required final approval authority
Over US$500 million (encouraged or permitted industry)	Final approval from State Council
Over US$100 million (restricted industry)	
Over US$100 million (encouraged or permitted industry)	MOFCOM and NDRC
Over US$50 million (restricted industry)	
Less than US$100 million (encouraged or permitted industry)	MOFTEC
Less than US$50 million (restricted industry)	

C. Devonshire-Ellis et al. (eds.), *Mergers & Acquisitions in China*, China Briefing, DOI: 10.1007/978-3-642-14919-1_4, © Asia Briefing Ltd. 2011

General Procedures

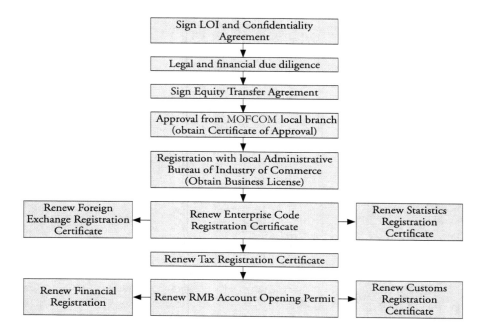

Equity Transaction

An equity acquisition will involve the transfer or subscription of the registered capital of the target company and be subject to a thorough review from MOFCOM.

Thus, an equity acquisition will require the following documentation:

- the unanimous shareholders resolution of the target domestic company (LLC or JSLC) on the contemplated equity acquisition;
- application for the converting establishment of the FIE;
- contract and articles of association of the FIE to be formed after acquisition;
- the agreement on the foreign investor's acquisition of equities of shareholders of the domestic company or on its subscription of the capital increase of the target domestic companies;
- audit report on the financial statement of the previous fiscal year of the target domestic company;
- the notarized and certified documents for the foreign investor's identity, registration and credit standing;
- the descriptions about the enterprises invested in by the target domestic enterprise;
- duplicates of the business licenses of the target domestic enterprise;

1 The Acquisition Procedure

- the proposal of employees arrangement in the target domestic enterprise;
- documents relevant to the agreements on liabilities of the domestic company, appraisal report issued by an appraisal institution and disclosure and explanations for the associated transaction, if applicable;
- other documents related to the following may be required: business scope and scale, etc.

Equity acquisitions by foreign investors may be carried out through an indirect offshore acquisition or as a direct onshore acquisition. PRC law also permits existing FIEs to make equity acquisitions if certain conditions are satisfied.

Asset Acquisition

When setting up asset acquisitions, a foreign investor must either establish a new FIE (usually a WFOE) which purchases and operates the assets, or buy the assets and inject them into a new or existing FIE.

An asset acquisition will require the following documentation:

- the resolution of the property rights holders or governing body of the domestic enterprise on the consent of the sale of the assets;
- the application for the establishment of the post-acquisition FIE;
- contract and articles of association of the FIE to be established;
- the asset purchase agreement signed by the foreign-funded enterprise to be established and the domestic enterprise, or by the foreign investor and the domestic enterprise;
- the articles of association and the business license (duplicate) of the target company;
- the creditor notification issued by the target company and the creditor's statement on the contemplated acquisition;
- the notarized and certified documents for the identity, registration and credit standing of the foreign investor;
- the proposal to arrange employees in the target domestic enterprise;
- the documents relevant to the target company's liabilities arrangement, appraisal report and disclosures and explanations made by the parties to the acquisition;
- other documents related to the following may be required: permit/license obtained for the contemplated asset acquisition.

A PRC acquisition vehicle is usually established at the same time as the acquisition to permit the operation of the assets. A great deal of government liaison work may be necessary for this type of transaction and the auditors' notification is sometimes required. Worker settlement arrangements are also required and examined in the approval process; sometimes formal consultations with the target's workers are also requested.

Merger

Some key points to note include:

- will be generally approved by the original Approval Authority of the relevant FIE;
- registration procedure should be carried out with SAIC or local counterparts;
- should a merger be capable of creating industry monopolies or market dominance over specific commodities or services, it will be subject to antitrust review and scrutiny by the authorities;
- if the target company is to be dissolved in the merger, then all creditors must be notified within 10 days of receiving an initial approval reply from the approval authority according to the PRC liquidation and dissolution procedures;
- it is subjected to a multi-step approval process with preliminary approvals required from both the surviving and dissolving entities' approval authorities and a final approval required from the surviving entity's approval authority;
- when the merger involves more than one competent authority, it has to be approved by the appropriate authority having jurisdiction over the post-merger FIE. Following the approval, relevant registration procedures should be carried out with the SAIC or its local counterparts;
- pre-approval review for possible impact on competition in China is required if the assets or revenues in China exceed specified thresholds.

Key Issues

- All documents submitted for review must be translated into Chinese; some authenticated translations will be required depending on the local practice.
- Approvals generally require 30 days but a number of factors (such as size, approval level, locality etc.) may have a significant affect on the approval time period.
- Any amendments to the registration or company particulars must be filed with the competent AIC and updated appropriately.
- The purchase price must be based on a third party appraisal of the assets or equity interest acquired.
- Pre-approval review for possible effects on competition in China is required if the assets or revenues of either or both parties in China exceed specified thresholds.

Due Diligence

1 Operational Due Diligence

Chinese enterprises often lack useful and reliable operational information and some transactions have not lived up to acquirers' expectations after the discovery of operational surprises or weaknesses. The likelihood of buyers being disappointed by the performance of the target company can be reduced by conducting Operational Due Diligence (ODD).

ODD can be a highly effective tool in helping the buyer understand exactly how the target company works, which in turn leads to a trouble free transition after the consummation of the acquisition. It can also prove effective at assisting the buyer in evaluating how well the target's current operations support the future strategic objectives. ODD should include a detailed assessment of the following:

- the functional operations of the target and the processes and systems supporting it;
- the inter-connectedness of these operations;
- the likely impact of operations on the future financial value of the company.

ODD completes the view of the target company in areas not fully addressed by financial due diligence and can often be a very important tool in identifying the real value of the transaction. Financial due diligence typically merely verifies the target company's financial statement and attempts to opine on the potential future sales and profitability, but chiefly uses historic patterns and trends as its base point. ODD goes much deeper in assessing the target company's functional operations and the interactions between them. The insights gained in this process can often determine a significant amount of the transaction's value, or lack of it.

ODD can be used at various stages in the acquisition process, but is typically used to achieve one or more of the following outcomes.

C. Devonshire-Ellis et al. (eds.), *Mergers & Acquisitions in China*, China Briefing, DOI: 10.1007/978-3-642-14919-1_5, © Asia Briefing Ltd. 2011

Target Assessment

Identifying potential operational enhancement upside opportunities, along with the key commercial issues associated with the deal. The unforeseen opportunities that might deliver say, an extra US$10 million to the bottom line. When factored into a valuation of say, ten times cash-flow, such an uplift translates into an sizeable US$100 million of additional value. That can be the edge a buyer needs to place a deal winning bid in a competitive bidding process.

Bid Evaluation

- Reviewing management structures and controls and providing an assessment of operational effectiveness and benchmarking the business against other similar businesses.
- Identification and validation of any assumed operational improvement initiatives that underpin the target's business plan and assessment of the business's capability to deliver each initiative. ODD will identify the deal killers— aggressive management plans that simply would not fly.

Post Deal

Highlighting operational areas where improvements can be made to enhance productivity and profitability and work with the management team to accelerate the improvement process.

Establishment

One of the most fundamental issues that needs to be verified in operational due diligence is whether a target company or potential partner has been properly established and is legally existing. This is especially true if the target is an FIE, as special attention needs to be paid towards compliance of the target business to verification, approval and registration procedures of an FIE. Documents which need to be checked include:

- current and former business licenses;
- investment project proposal as well as the feasibility study;
- constitutional documents of the company—in the case of JV's this would include the joint venture contract itself as well as other articles of association;
- verification documents issued by the NDRC or any of its subsidiaries (if applicable);

1 Operational Due Diligence   39

- approval documents—in the case of FIEs this would include the MOFTEC approval letter and the accompanying approval certificate;
- other registration documents as issued by the appropriate government authorities and pursuant to the applicable laws and regulations. This would include tax registration as well as foreign exchange registration;
- documents relating to the contribution of capital—for FIEs this includes the valuation certificate which relates to in-kind contributions, the capital contribution verification report, and copies of the investment certificates that are issued to each investor by the FIE;
- asset valuation reports—these must be ratified;
- any documents that give evidence to any transfer of equity interest or shares;
- documents evidencing any increase or decrease of registered capital and/or the total amount of investment;
- documents that supply evidence to equity interest or shares being used as securities;
- documents evidencing any bank accounts operated by the potential target;
- any other documents pertaining to approvals, licenses or permits required for the establishment and operation of the target company.

Take note that the examination of any of these documents should be done so whilst taking into consideration the context of other documents. This should allow for a full understanding of the target company's overall situation.

Organizational Structure

The organizational structure is a key point for the operational success of the target business. Details that need to be checked in regard to due diligence in this matter are:

- all investors or shareholders in the target business, as well as the governmental departments in charge of them;
- the company's external organization structure. This includes the details of all domestic and overseas subsidiaries, representative offices, branches, distribution centers, research operations and other associated enterprises together with the appropriate documents evidencing their proper establishment and operations;
- the company's internal organizational structure with an organizational chart disclosing the full names, age, remuneration and contract details of the members of any supervisory board, board of directors, senior management and other key personnel;
- any company manuals or internal company rules or policies;
- documentary evidence pertaining to all of the above, including copies of business licenses, constitutional documents (such as shareholder agreements), JV contracts and articles of association, government approvals and registration documents;

- other documentary evidence including minutes of all meetings of the company organs and adopted resolutions from the last 3 years, as well as letters of appointment and employment agreements.

Chinese authorities are also cracking down on outbound–inbound investment, where Chinese businesses or even individuals would establish a business entity outside of China with the sole purpose of re-investing in China from offshore. In this way they may take advantage of something which is also available to foreign investors, and dispose easily of the off shore holding entity after onshore assets have been transferred to its onshore subsidiary at a well-below market price. Legislative bodies have imposed heavy restrictions on this practice and as such, special attention and legality is required when any offshore business is involved.

Risk Assessment

Risk assessment is vital. The four main categories of operational risk by international standards are: (1) process-related, (2) people-related, (3) systems-related and, (4) external events. These are qualitative problems that can have a significant quantitative impact, and they tend to be the instigators of the conditions for the most serious mismanagement and endemic corporate corruption. ODD aims to assess the possibilities of these risks and their potential effects on the business before an acquirer makes their bid.

ODD analysis into risk assessment can lead the acquiring business into proactively implementing a number of strategies at the time of acquisition, thus avoiding any impact or loss from one (or more) of the above risk categories. Acquiring or merging enterprises may look at accounting audits, regulatory reviews, employee training programs and background checks, data security, contingency planning and the implementation of a code of conduct as just a few methods of negating such risks.

Key Operational Functions

A company's operational capabilities can be the basis of a deal and specific auditing tests must be devised in order to measure the value chain. The steps involved will vary depending upon the company being considered for investment, but should involve an on-site analysis of the target's daily business processes and of the systems supporting the business' operations. This analysis should involve an evaluation of production capacity, raw material flows, inventory levels and all other factors that are necessary for the business to conduct normal operations.

ODD may also assist in assessing the possibilities and, from an operational point of view, administrative advantages of merging or centralizing already existing independent operations of the target business. How this is done is unique to each situation, however, if you have let us say, a combination of JVs, WFOEs and ROs, then it may make a lot of sense to try and bring all these into one holding operation in China for ease of management.

Environmental Considerations

As the Chinese government becomes more and more concerned about the environmental issues in China and the damage that polluting companies cause, it is taking decisive steps to regulate and to ensure compliance with environmental standards. As a result, M&A requires very conscientious due diligence with regard to environmental liabilities. For example, a factory that has been polluting the local rivers for some 20 years may one day get prosecuted for massive damages.

To avoid the risk of getting involved in M&A activities that might end up a disaster, in the due diligence context, attention should be paid to the following information:

- What is the current environmental situation of the company?

  - Has it had any environmental problems in the past or might it cause any environmental problems in the future after the take-over?
  - If yes, then what kind of counter-measures have been taken and what are the results of these?
  - Has the company stored or used any hazardous substances, raw materials, objects etc., or has it been involved in any hazardous procedures?
  - Has the company paid any pollutant discharge fees over the last years?

- What is the company's policy regarding environmental issues?
- Can the company provide any documentary evidence regarding information such as environmental impact assessments, licenses, approvals, permits, permissions, certificates, applications, registrations and notifications?
- Can the company provide any reports on its environmental situation produced by (private and governmental) third parties over the last 5 years?

The environment is still a developing issue in China. Expect over the next few years that regulations will become tighter and more strictly enforced, thus requiring further attention to due diligence.

2 Financial Due Diligence

Copies of filed accounts can be difficult to extract from the target business. This is largely due to the fact that many businesses in China operate two sets of books—one internal, which shows their true position, and one official, that shows their "official" position. This is, of course, illegal but is a common practice as tax avoidance in China is rife due to the high level of profits tax Chinese companies have to pay. The State Administration of Tax is also woefully inefficient at making collections. Some of the SAT's practices—such as making VAT liable on invoicing, not on collection—have also led to inappropriate financial reporting being the norm in many Chinese companies.

This means that the official set of books as presented to the Chinese authorities and audited may not represent the true strength of the company, which can put the Chinese partner in a quandary about how to disclose an official, but financially poor, set of books to you, the potential partner, yet at the same time admit to keeping a second set, with its obvious sensitive overtones?

Assessing Financial Statements and Audits

As mentioned above, get in a professional accounting practice that has experience of conducting work with SOEs to assess the quality of the audited accounts as presented. A two to three day site visit by an experienced, impartial auditor should be enough to provide an opinion on whether accounts and financial statements presented to you are indeed a true statement of fact or whether there are areas within them that warrant further investigation or explanation.

This needs to be handled with care and understanding. If it is purely a business assessment that needs to be made as to the viability of the partner, then to some extent a pragmatic approach to the Chinese parties reporting methodology may be taken provided this would not impact on your JV at a later stage. If a valuation is carried out then this becomes a much more complex issue with far more serious implications.

Note: Chinese Listed Companies in Hong Kong only averaged a score of 44 out of 100 in corporate governance and transparency issues in a fairly recent survey conducted by the Hong Kong City University. You must get in someone to check that what you are being told—even if they are presenting Chinese audited accounts—is correct.

It is also vitally important to ensure that these same practices are NOT carried over into your own business, because:

- the SAT places all Foreign Invested Enterprises in China (which includes Joint Ventures) under Category 1, the highest in tax bureau monitoring and assessments. You cannot afford to have a lack of accounting transparency;
- the Chinese Tax Bureau can levy up to five times the amount of any tax not paid in late payment penalties;

It is advisable to appoint a CPA firm to conduct an "Asset Appraisal Report" on your target's business that will give you a more realistic picture. This should not be conducted from the target's usual accountants, so that at the very least you will be given a clear picture as to where the discrepancies lie between internal and official sets of books. An "Asset Appraisal Report" should be conducted in the final stage of the transaction when two parties bargain the price and this CPA firm should be appointed by both parties.

Due diligence would be required to obtain details and documentation regarding the following:

- RMB and foreign currency loans, including shareholder loans;
- outstanding indebtedness, such as bonds;
- securities provided by the company to third parties or by third parties to the company in relation to any debts the company has.

China Compliance: Financial and Secretarial

It is vital to be, and to remain in compliance in both accounting and the corporate secretarial (documentation) aspects of your business. A lack of attention to detail in your paperwork alone can seriously jeopardize your operations.

Corporate Secretarial

- Trademarks/patents: ensure that they have been registered in China, and where the ownership lies. We've seen agents registering their clients marks as their own IP.
- Business licenses: all pertinent licenses and permits – export licenses, customs and SAFE (foreign currency) registrations and so on – need to be renewed periodically. If you don't know what you are looking at, outsource this to someone who does and will take care of renewals for you on an impartial basis.

Taxes and Tax Filings

Most filings need to be conducted on a monthly basis, (Business Tax, VAT, IIT; except CIT which is on a quarterly basis) and audits annually. If you are not conducting such filings—you are not in compliance. Outsource this or get in at least quarterly checks to ensure all is in place and where it should be. Reporting also should be to a professional standard and maintained. An inability to provide accounts, audited accounts or on-going documentation is a sign that all is not well. Ensure your reporting and checking systems are in place and if necessary hire a firm to provide the impartial monitoring you need.

Taxes that need to be considered in due diligence include:

- Corporate Income Tax (CIT).
- VAT—a turnover tax at 17%, reduced rates are available in certain situations.
- Consumption Tax—additional turnover tax placed on luxury goods.
- Business Tax—applicable to services not subject to VAT.

- Land Value-Added Tax.
- Resource Tax.
- Urban Real-Estate Tax.
- Stamp Duty.
- Motor Vehicle and Vessel Acquisition Tax—including taxes on usage and license plates.
- Deed Tax—imposed on acquisition of land use rights and real property.
- Individual Income Tax (IIT)

Other tax related issues to consider include:

- taxes to be paid during the usual operation of business, including applicable rates, exemptions, and reductions;
- import/export duties to be paid during business operation including applied rates as well as any exemptions or reductions that are available or currently obtained. Illegally negating import duties has been a common practice among Chinese businesses in the past, so be wary;
- any outstanding tax, import or export liabilities that the business may have
- pending and/or expected disputes in regards to the above issues
- documents supporting the above points, including previous tax returns for the last 7 years, governmental registration, approval and permission documents in relation to preferential tax rates and/or exemptions, and documentary evidence regarding the payment of import/export duties.

Dilution

It pays to be diligent in both knowing a target's future movements and intentions— other than the acquisition—as well as your own contractual arrangements, as dilution is a major way in which you could loose your grip on the target after having acquired a percentage in it. The issuance of new shares is one such way of diluting a foreign investor's equity interests of their newly acquired targets. Despite PRC laws preventing two consecutive share issues within a year of each other, it is more than likely that your investments in the FIE or JV are likely to last more than 12 months or even several years. These current laws also prevent foreign companies from purchasing A shares issued to the public, thus giving the target an ideal way to dilute your investments. Be wary, because should you be on the income tax threshold, a substantial public share issuance can potentially dilute your own investments and could have large financial setbacks.

Problems?

If your local staff or partner is late in filings, reporting, or is reluctant or unable to fully explain the financial or documentary aspects of the office or business, be wary. Accounting is either being handled properly or it isn't. It is important to ensure any problems are nipped in the bud and dealt with. Lack of training and incompetence over money can be dealt with by outsourcing or getting in someone qualified. Fraud and non-compliance are far more serious and need to be stopped. Usually a one-two day site visit by an experienced external accountant is enough to identify whether there are actually problems and the likely extent of these. From there an action plan can be formulated, the issues explored, corrected and the business put back on a compliant platform.

3 Legal Due Diligence

Acquiring assets requires conscientious due diligence, but acquiring state-owned assets and state-owned enterprises in China requires extra special scrutiny. Until recently, M&A activity had not grown very fast in China, but the liberalizations unleashed after China's WTO entry are gradually easing some of the restrictions and have begun to kindle stronger interest in acquiring Chinese assets.

China's state sector is opening up now to M&A activity that foreigners can participate in, as well as to the sale of bad loans and settled assets by the Chinese banks. New state asset exchanges are being set up across the country, and state organizations (such as the Shanghai government) are beginning to offload their SOE shares onto the market.

It is worthy to note that, in submitting legal applications to the relevant authorities during the acquisition process, the laws binding these processes are Chinese, and basic legal due diligence would ensure that these applications are submitted in Chinese.

Procedures and Due Diligence in Acquiring State-Owned Enterprises Initial Steps: Letters of Intent

Usually, the Chinese party will approach the foreign investor or potential investor with a draft "letter of intent" or "memorandum of understanding" outlining the fact that the two parties are going to discuss the matter and laying out the complete procedures for doing so up to the actual share transfer. It is wise to pay some attention to these and be quite sure about what you are committing to. Often, the Chinese side will be somewhat aggressive in their approach. The sage investor will limit any commitment to 'reviewing valuations', and then base a decision to proceed further or not on that report. Essentially, however, these letters exist to ensure both parties are on the same page as regards the process, and to try and keep potential misunderstandings to a minimum. But pay attention to them and do not commit too much too soon.

Asset Valuations

These must be conducted by a valuation firm licensed to conduct such work in China. There are a handful of international firms with trained personnel who have this ability to conduct such work to correct procedures, and a large number of Chinese firms. However, many Chinese businesses will request that their local auditor conducts the valuation.

There are also issues as to who pays for valuations. Local firms are generally cheap (often fees are based on a commission element which excludes any impartiality), while the international firms are more expensive. Cheaper firms equate to cheaper valuations which usually means higher acquisition costs for the investor. The matter of who pays for the valuation can be a sticking point—usually the foreign investor will have to stump up the bill, especially if an international firm is used. However, who pays is up to the parties and this can be negotiated. Justifying to the Chinese partner about using an international firm is easy: "We are an international business and we require an international firm we know." If your supplier can conduct such work in China then the Chinese party should have no problem with that. If they do—be wary.

It is wise at this point to appoint a firm to conduct due diligence work. This includes legal work in identifying that documentation is present and correct, for examples see below.

Land Use Rights Title

Two types of land use exist. Allocated rights effectively equate to land rental; they are issued to the venture for a period of years but only give the rights to use the land. This would mean that any buildings erected on the land will benefit the land-owner rather than the company, and also gives the landowner the right to throw you off the land should the Chinese partner default on the rental.

Granted rights are more similar to land ownership than rental, however these too are only issued for a period of years. The difference is you are given the title to the land for this period of time, which means you can profit from the sale of the rights later on. This is particularly useful if you intend on making considerable long term investments on the land, or wish to use the rights as security to raise loans. When injecting land into part of JV equity, be sure that it is granted land use rights, otherwise the contribution is virtually meaningless.

It is important that you check the mortgages and other encumbrances, building insurances, third parties rights and actual or potential litigation issues in relation to your potential premises, as well as any documentation regarding all sites and buildings occupied by the company and any of its subsidiaries—both domestic and overseas.

Land Use Rights Scope

This is very important. It is been the cause of many scandals—are the rights to the land actually for the purpose of your business activities? Land use comes under close scrutiny in China, with areas of land designated for specific purposes or industries (e.g. farming manufacturing etc.) by the central government, and all land use requiring state-level approval. Many a deal has been done with land actually earmarked for agricultural use being offloaded at a premium to investors expecting to be able to build a factory. China has 20% of the world's population and 5% of its arable land. Getting agricultural use land converted to factory land is a massive, almost unsolvable problem. Make sure your land comes with the scope you expect.

Rights of Access

Will this be granted if you have access via someone else's land?

Intellectual Property Rights

There are still large problems—from a foreign point of view—with regards to China's intellectual property laws and particularly the lax enforcement of these regulations. Be extremely vigilant when checking the status of all your trademarks, patents, copyrights, software and enterprise names in China. This would also include rights owned by third parties but used by the business on the basis of license agreements or even without contractual basis, as well as those owned by the business but used by a third party with or without contractual agreement or license.

Confirmation that You Can Continue Your Business as a 100% Foreign-Invested Enterprise

Some businesses have restrictions on the amount of equity a foreign party can have. Make sure it is permitted for you to have the equity balance you want. Also clarify on the legal establishment of the target company.

Anti-trust Provisions

China's anti-trust laws are still somewhat unclear and may require specialist review. The laws would generally only apply to large scale acquisitions, but in niche markets it is also quite applicable due to the percentage of market share you stand to gain.

Make sure your acquisition is not in breach of these provisions, or if it is, you do so according to the parameters that allows such acquisitions to take place. MOFCOM and SAIC do have the power to deny your acquisition should you be seen to be in breach, and in the very least you will be asked to produce a report which is likely to cost valuable time and money. Also look to clarify any details regarding current, pending or possible anti-trust matters that the target has been or may be involved in, and any documentary evidence supporting this.

Are all aspects of the business in place that you expect? Did the Chinese company sub-contract out any of it is work? Make sure you know exactly what you are buying.

Legal Proceedings

Due diligence is needed to examine and clarify any actual and/or potential legal proceedings. This involves obtaining the details of civil, criminal or administrative litigation, arbitration or mediation proceedings in China or abroad involving the target company and all of its subsidiaries. Government orders or any other decisions of a government authority relating to the business or its subsidiaries, which have been received in the last 3 years are also required.

Make sure that there are also no pending awards that have been rendered against the company, which have not yet been fully executed; if there are, consult the company's legal representatives regarding any possible outcomes.

Memorandum of Understanding (MOU)

It is common practice in negotiations within China to introduce a Memorandum of Understanding (MOU). While this is technically not a legally binding document, it does outline and clarify the position of each party in documenting the mutual understanding of each others' positions, so be thorough. They tend to act as a basic draft for the later JV contract and articles, so it is important not to undervalue its importance. If there is any change in a documented agreement, the Chinese side will want to know why and will often refer back to any items identified within a MOU.

Miscellaneous Issues

There are also other practical issues to consider as well, such as:

1. Employment issues—following an acquisition it may be the case that some employee transfers take place between the target business and the acquirer, which would be subject to Article 26 of the PRC Labor Law. However, it is also

necessary to review the terms of the Labor Contract Law which came into effect from January 1, 2008 (more details can be found in Chap. 9). Termination of employee contracts during acquisition results in compensation according to the number of working years an employee has amassed. Termination of employment contracts after the acquisition shall be also subject to the total working years prior to the acquisition. An FIE, however, has no obligation to hire any employees of the target company.

With a merger, the employment contracts of all employees will automatically be transferred to the post-merger FIE and would not result in severance. Any amendments or cancellations to contracts shall only take place with the employee's consent, which would generally require a redundancy package, at the cost of the business.

In all acquisitions, the investor should make sure all payments and contributions have been made to the employees such as individual income tax and social insurance. Meanwhile, the purchaser should ensure that all employment contracts are checked for non-compete and confidentially obligations that could give rise to liability on his or the employees part.

2. All disputes between an employee and employer are subject to labor arbitration procedures before court proceedings may take place.

3. Inheriting staff—you can pick up the entire welfare and pensions burden of SOE personnel if they are transferred over to your company, backdated to the day they started work for the SOE. Take professional advice over this issue or you may end up inheriting a massive burden.

4. Contracts—look into all contracts worth more than RMB100,000 or 5% of the business's net assets, this would also include employment contracts, insurance, or any other material contract that is essential for the operation of the business and any of its subsidiaries.

5. Are liabilities clean? Get a binding statement that liabilities not part of your acquisition agreement, incurred up to the date of the acquisition, are to be borne by the Chinese side and not you.

6. Assessing financial statements and auditing asset valuers: get in a professional accounting practice that has experience of conducting work with SOE's to assess the quality of the audited accounts as presented.

7. Negotiating the valuation: there is some flexibility in negotiating the valuation, often with issues that are unique to the specific case. Frank and cordial discussions with the Chinese side can often lead to breakthroughs via balancing various issues in different ways.

Finally, are all aspects of the business in place that you expect? Did the Chinese company sub-contract out any of it is work? Make sure you know exactly what you are buying.

Assets Supervision and Administration Commissions and Asset Exchange Centers

Once an acquisition fee has been agreed at the subsidiary level, the Chinese side will need to make a proposal to its own Parent SOE in order to have the sale ratified by the main board. Depending upon specific circumstances, this will also need to be filed at either the SASAC or the local State-Owned Assets Exchange Centre.

Public Bidding and Auction

Once an acquisition fee has been agreed upon and approved, the target is given 20 days of public bidding to analyze and/or accept rival bids from other businesses. These rival bids are quite uncommon, and if the original acquirer possesses the right of first refusal they can raise their offer. Some diligence is required here as there are ways for acquirers to restrict the target's likelihood of accepting a rival offer through negotiating terms in the original acquisition contract. But be careful—and this is where due diligence plays its part—as over-restrictive measures by the acquirer can be in violation of China's M&A regulations. It would also pay to remember that those making the decisions for the target business have a responsibility to get the best acquisition deal, and that the Chinese authorities are becoming more suspicious towards under-valued acquisitions. This can potentially be a testing phase for the acquirer, but if due diligence has played its part thoroughly, then you can be confident that you will secure the deal.

Concluding the Transfer

At this point, administration takes over, with a variety of different procedures to go through depending upon how the acquisition was structured. Paperwork confirming the transfer also needs to be raised and filed with the MOFCOM on the share transfer, with additional filings at the local Administration of Industry and Commerce; together with newly drafted articles and applications for a new WFOE business license and various other mandatory registrations.

Valuing an Acquisition Target

1 Overview

As mentioned above, the Ministry of Commerce implemented the *Rules on the Merger with and Acquisition of Domestic Enterprises by Foreign Investors* in September 2006 which aim to further increase corporate transparency, cut back on the practice of "round-tripping" by Chinese companies looking to benefit from incentives offered to foreign investors, as well as strengthen the mechanism by which foreign firms are supervised in their acquisition of domestic enterprises.

One regulation is the requirement of the employment of an outside asset appraisal organ and the use of the subsequent appraisal as a basis for the determination of the transaction price. The essential parts of the provision are as follows:

- parties to acquisition (both equity and asset related) must determine price on the basis of the equity interest to be transferred or assets to be sold as assessed by an asset appraisal organ;
- parties are prohibited from transferring equity interest or selling assets at a price "obviously lower" than the assessed value;
- all foreign firms involved in M&A with a domestic enterprise must seek outside asset appraisal organs;
- asset appraisal of non-SOE is to be conducted using internationally accepted appraisal standards;
- asset appraisal of SOE is subject to state-owned asset appraisal regulations.

Because the result of the asset appraisal is to establish the reference price for the transaction, the valuation process is one that foreign investors will want to begin early and remain involved in throughout.

C. Devonshire-Ellis et al. (eds.), *Mergers & Acquisitions in China*, China Briefing, DOI: 10.1007/978-3-642-14919-1_6, © Asia Briefing Ltd. 2011

Investors will want to begin their own asset valuation processes before commencing the process through a third party. This will give foreign investors an idea of what they are willing to pay, as well as providing a yardstick by which to measure the effectiveness of the independent asset evaluator.

2 Valuation Techniques

Valuation of Non-SOEs

Appraisal of non-SOEs is to be conducted by an approved asset appraisal organ, using internationally accepted accounting standards. A potential acquirer of a domestic Chinese enterprise should perform its own valuation of the business to establish the price range which they are willing to pay for the target business. Financial due diligence should also be performed prior to the appraiser's valuation as it will play a key role in identifying factors impacting the acquirer's valuation model as well as identifying opportunities to present evidence to the authorized appraiser which may influence the appraiser's valuation before it is finalized.

Some points to consider:

- there is no single universal valuation method that provides an appropriate value in every case as each target has unique characteristics that need to be considered;
- in practice it is usually better to apply several different techniques and then compare the results as this will usually reveal the factors which are adding or destroying value;
- in addition to valuing a target on a stand alone basis it is also necessary to consider how much the target will be worth to the acquirer as a whole after the transaction is completed;
- a discounted cash flow method is often used as it takes into account future benefits to the acquirer, however, this method has its problems, for example, China's expanding economy makes predictions of cash flows complicated and agreeing on an appropriate discount rate is not as straightforward a process as in more developed economies; potential buyers should use sensible calculation methods and make sure they are accepted in advance by the decision makers.

Other valuation techniques may include:

- an analysis of comparable transactions in a similar industry;
- an asset valuation focused on replacement cost;
- a Greenfield analysis.

Again there may be difficulties, therefore, the application of several techniques and subsequent comparison is strongly advised.

2 Valuation Techniques

Valuation of SOEs

SOEs are generally valued at the net assets value, which equals to total assets minus total liabilities. As a result, valuations of SOEs for investment purposes tend to be inaccurate and prejudiced. Local auditors are torn by conflicts of interest between their government sponsors and the government-related firms they assess.

The due diligence for the real value of the state-owned assets is, therefore, very important. All SOE assets have to be re-appraised by some appointed state assets appraisal companies before the sale. Most foreign buyers will still hire their own accounting firms to go through the books.

Assets valuation for SOEs generally consists of valuation by six categories of appraiser: "assets valuation" by certified assets appraiser; "real-estate valuation" by registered real-estate appraiser; "land valuation" by land appraiser; "mining rights valuation" by mining rights appraiser; "insurance survey and loss adjustment" by insurance surveyors and loss adjusters; and "used vehicle valuation" by the used vehicle appraiser.

There are two measures for valuing assets, namely nominal assets valuation or integral assets valuation. If nominal, according to specific and different objectives, valuation purpose and valuation implementation conditions, the replacement cost method, market comparison method, income method and liquidation price method (valuation for non-performing assets or bankrupt liquidation of the enterprise) may be adopted. For the integral assets valuation, the asset-based valuation method is the main option. In recent years, the income method (primarily the discounted cash flow method) has been applied gradually. The market comparison is another option, but has been relatively less adopted due to the difficulties in obtaining the comparisons and comparison adjustments.

Main valuation methods taken by the registered real-estate appraiser for the real-estate valuation include: comparable approach, cost approach, income approach, method of long-term trend, etc. These valuation approaches are similar to the practices of the Hong Kong Real Estate Surveyor.

Main valuation methods taken by the domestic land appraisers for the land include: income approach, cost approach, comparable approach, residue approach, etc.

The insurance assets valuation carried out by the insurance surveyors and loss adjusters are mainly based on the methods of replacement cost approach and comparable approach.

The enterprise assets valuation (mainly for mining resource assets) carried out by the mining right appraiser are normally based on the following methods: replacement cost approach, geoscience sorting method, discounted cash flow method, comparable approach, etc.

The nominal assets valuation carried out by the used vehicle appraiser are mainly based on the following methods: market approach, income approach, liquidation price method and replacement cost method, which are basically similar to the methods adopted by the certified assets appraiser.

3 Potential Problems in Accurate Asset Valuation

Asset appraisal in China must be approached with additional care as there are many more China-specific factors that may play a vital role in estimating value. There are a number of problems to overcome, as follows.

Quality Information

The quality and accuracy of valuation is heavily dependent upon the quality and accuracy of the information and data upon which it is based. In more developed countries there is a multitude of information available to help valuers better understand the enterprise, the industry, and relevant market conditions, including published studies, market research papers, annual company reports and other publicly available information.

However, China's relatively young economy lacks such reliable, independent, quality information. Various problems that foreign firms have encountered include: firms keeping two sets of books, maintaining poor accounting records, having high volume of off-book sales, failing to make a distinction between corporate and personal funds, lack of understanding of basic accounting principles, and inability to provide a satisfactory estimate of production capacity.

Also due to China's relatively young market economy, it is difficult for valuations to be officially checked against market price. China comparisons are also difficult, as indicators and benchmarks which are only 2 years old may not be the best signs of the current economic and financial situation in China.

Accounting Standards

The Ministry of Finance (MOF) has worked hard to reduce the gap between Chinese and international accounting standards. Since 1997, eight regulations on accounting practices have been passed. The latest Accounting Standards for Business Enterprises came into effect in January 1, 2007, which standardized the accounting treatment for different industries. But the MOF still has much to do before China's accounting procedures can fully meet international standards. There are clearly a number of issues to overcome, such as possible fraudulent transactions, etc.

Contingent and Hidden Liabilities

Some Chinese companies may display a few shortcomings in regards to regulatory compliance, and as a result may accumulate significant tax and other liabilities over time. Should these liabilities be exposed in a timely fashion, correct adjustments can be made to the overall assessment of the value of the asset. However, such liabilities may be buried deep within the accounting books and may not be readily apparent.

In the case of asset acquisitions, it is necessary to verify legal ownership of the domestic enterprise's assets. It should also be verified that the domestic enterprise's assets can be legally transferred, and that they have not been used as collateral against any loans or liabilities the domestic enterprise has incurred, especially because in China it is common for a third party's property to be included in the company's books.

Equity acquisition is faced with a higher degree of risk, owing to hidden financial burdens such as loans, debts and bad inventories, and human resource issues such as unpaid social security, employee income taxes, labor contract clauses and labor disputes.

In order to identify key risk areas, firms should focus on specific characteristics of the asset in question, including, for example, the nature of the industry, the characteristics of key management, etc.

Intangible Assets

The valuation of intangible assets is always a difficult task, and is a recent concept in China. Intangibles are amortized using the straight-line method over their useful lives and no more than 10 years, whereas standard international practice tends to allow for a 20 year amortization process. Intangible assets must be valued on an annual basis, and if the book value is greater than their recoverable value, they are required to provide for the devaluation. Intangible assets the useful lives of which cannot be determined cannot be amortized. R&D costs incurred before legally obtaining an intangible asset such as a patent, if any R&D costs arise, must be expensed in the period in which they are incurred. In addition, the valuation of intellectual property must be taken into consideration.

Issues in Conducting Asset Valuation
for State-Owned Enterprises

The management of state-owned enterprise valuation is dictated by the different classes of government managing the businesses—central, provincial, local city and county.

The Land and Resources Commission of the State Council is mainly in charge of the administration of more than 190 large enterprises including solely state-owned and state-holding industrial and commercial enterprises. Financial enterprises are managed by the Ministry of Finance, the provincial state resource committee supervises state-owned provincial enterprises, the local city's state resource committee supervises the state-owned local enterprises and the county committees supervise state-owned county enterprises. However, if the project is for listing, the valuing report is managed by the Land and Resources Commission of the State Council irrespective of the current management.

Most of the valuation for domestic SOEs is for restructuring of the stockholding or listing on the stock market, acquisition, mergers, and reorganization. Generally, valuation is of all the assets (fixed and current). So the biggest differences between domestic and international valuation work is that connection between the book value of the current enterprise's assets and the valuation must be established.

Before valuation, a certified accountant carries out a financial audit and the audited book value is deemed as the pre-valuation value. Since the registered assets valuer evaluates all assets (fixed and current), some accounting knowledge and approaches are required and it is difficult for property valuers from overseas to comply with the specific demands of the valuation of the current assets of state owned enterprises unless they have accounting expertise or work with a partner.

It should be noted that the National Securities Committee and National Capital Committee usually demand that the depreciated replacement cost (DRC) should be applied for the valuation of tangible assets for state-owned enterprises listed overseas (they have however just approved the use of income method). PRC valuation experts rarely understand obsolescence and this is one area—the application of obsolescence in DRC calculations—that international valuation experts demonstrate their abilities.

Choosing an Asset Valuation Firm

There are a handful of international firms and a large number of Chinese firms with trained personnel who have this ability to conduct such work. However, many Chinese businesses will request that their local auditor conducts the valuation as "they know the business".

In our experience in China, we strongly advise you to carry out extensive due diligence if choosing a local valuation firm. However, both local and international firms are capable of offering a good service. Nevertheless, problems can arise and there can also be issues as to who pays for valuations. While the international firms are more expensive, fees for accurate asset valuations may be worth the cost. If you are spending 5% on a RMB 50 million valuation, the money you save just in getting the real picture is worth the expenditure. Cheaper firms equate to cheaper valuations which usually means higher acquisition costs for the investor. In most cases, the evaluation firm will be jointly hired by the two parties involved and costs thus shared. But remember this still needs to be negotiated beforehand.

Mechanism for Purchase

Foreign investors can purchase Chinese SOEs through three avenues.

Firstly, the local assets and equity exchange. China's major municipal governments have gradually set up the exchanges to facilitate the trading of enterprises' assets and equity. Shanghai United Assets and Equity Exchange (http://new.suaee.com/suaee/portal/english/home.jsp) has also established an "express way" to streamline procedures for foreign investors. Projects valued under US$10 million will qualify for this express treatment. However, most exchange-listed projects are of a relatively small size.

Secondly, the match-making of the intermediaries. Most investment banks and financial consulting companies have up-to-date M&A information and they would provide value-added services in the process.

Thirdly, SOEs are often sold in the framework of the state holding corporations. Generally the state holding corporations will give a press conference in which they publicize a list of the SOEs they intend to sell. They also outline the preliminary structure of the sales. It can be buyouts, partial equity sales, debt-to-equity swap, sales of the assets, or expansion equity raising. There would be great flexibility in structuring, as the whole process is very dynamic and full of surprises. These state-holding corporations will sometimes hire a financial advisor to help the process, but most likely they will try handle it on their own. Therefore, it is in their interests to focus their efforts on only a few "very serious" buyers. Foreign investors have to show "serious" interest in obtaining detailed financial information.

It is worthwhile for the foreign investors to hire a Chinese intermediary in acquiring a SOE. They will provide valuable services and insights during the due diligence process. They can be critical in smoothing the relationships among buyers, shareholders, and the management. The advisors with strong government relations will also assist in tackling workers' pension problems, etc.

Foreign Exchange

China imposes strict rules governing cross-border foreign exchange transactions and places restrictions on the conversion of RMB into foreign currency. In particular, exchanges involving capital account items are strongly guarded and require approval from the SAFE. For current account foreign exchange transactions, the rules are generally less stringent. Nevertheless, during an M&A transaction, no matter whether equity or asset acquisition, approval from SAFE is necessary. Additionally, if an FIE borrows from an offshore entity to finance the deal then this type of loan must be registered with the SAFE.

4 Specific Issues in Business Acquisition and Reorganization from the Point of View of Appraisal

Explaining the Appraiser's Approach

China's appraisal industry is relatively new and is still developing. The introduction of worth/price-based theory will help to resolve the significant problems that have dogged China's assets appraisal industry and those relying on the results. Importantly, it will hopefully outweigh the strong emphasis placed on purely replacement costs used before and should effectively bridge the current gap between "values" and transaction prices. This change will be of great significance in improving the professionalism of China's appraisal industry, improving corporate governance, and satisfying the needs of an increasingly market focused economy.

Characteristics of China's Assets Appraisal Industry

Valuation approved by the State Council is under the administration of departments like the State Owned Assets Supervision and Administration Commission of the State Council, and so on. At the same time, valuation falls under the respective industrial and self discipline management of industrial associations, including the China Appraisal Society, China Institute of Real Estate Appraisers, China Real Estate Valuer Association and China Automobile Dealers Association. This leads to many anomalies including that valuers cannot be substituted by each other. Especially for assets valuation, real estate valuation and land valuation, the three areas can only be carried out at the same time by three different types of qualified valuers upon approval by the competent authorities from the three different industries.

If a state-owned business intends to list on the stock market, then valuations can only be completed by registered valuation institutions with securities business and certified assets appraiser qualifications. The land valuation can only be conducted by land valuation institutions with Class A and certified land valuers qualifications. If the purpose of enterprise valuation is for a mortgage loan, only an institution with the appropriate real estate valuation qualification and a real estate valuer will be authorized for this work.

In addition to all this, the operational scope of the real estate valuation institution and land valuation institution may fall into three different categories: Class A qualification, with which the institution may undertake valuation work throughout the entire country for all purposes, (Class A land valuation can be divided into Class A and Class A minus—institutions with Class A minus qualification may undertake valuation work throughout the entire country except for land valuation for stock market listing); Class B, with which the institution can operate within a province; Class C, with which the institution is only allowed to undertake valuation work at the local city level.

5 Characteristics of China's Assets Appraisal Standards

Since the 1990s, a large number of formative documents have been released successively concerning asset appraisal in China. In February 2004, the *Assets Appraisal Standards-Basic Standards* and the *Professional Ethics For Assets Appraisal-Basic Standards* were released.

The standard is guided by international appraisal theories and will give priority to conceptual regulations rather than detailed or inflexible regulations.

The valuation basis is an important part of asset appraisal theory in countries with a well-developed appraisal industry such as the USA and the UK. The identification and definition of valuation bases are promoted by the world's main appraisal standards, including the *International Valuation Standards*, the *Uniform Standards for Professional Appraisal Practice* of the USA and the *European Valuation Standards*, as the keys for determining appropriate appraised value. The same asset can have different values under different conditions, markets and purposes of appraisal, e.g. market value, investment value, liquidation value, insurance value, taxation value, etc. Under international standards appraisers should not use undefined value bases in their valuation work to avoid misleading readers and users of the appraisal report. Appraisers should always make clear if a non-market basis is used in a valuation, so that the users of the appraisal report will not deem it as the market value by misunderstanding. This concept is being adopted by China's appraisal regulatory and supervisory bodies but at a slow pace.

Attention is finally being paid to information disclosure within the appraisal industry as well as importance to the appraisal methodology. A number of serious problems have occurred in listed companies in particular due to improper and insufficient information disclosure in valuation reports. As a consequence, appraisal companies and governing bodies are setting out to change this legacy and appraisers are now required to fully disclose relevant information which will allow users of appraisal reports to understand and confidently use the appraisal results.

Finally, importance is being placed on educating users of appraisal reports to correctly understand and use reports—in this way a perceived failure of appraisal in China caused by misunderstanding or malignant use of the report users can be especially avoided.

6 Role of Assets Appraisal in Maintaining China's Stock Market Order

It has unfortunately been an occurrence for rogue managers in listed companies to damage the interests of investors and interfere in the normal running of the stock market. Accurate regular asset appraisal is one way to ensure fair and transparent criteria to judge the performance of a business. Appraisal can verify the transaction price in an asset reorganization and gives investors defined benchmarks. As such, this is a crucial area for maintaining a fair and orderly stock-market, shown by the requirements for regular independent valuations of property assets in most developed stock markets.

During the process of an asset restructuring or acquisition, an appraiser, acting as an independent professional, can give opinions regarding market value of the assets involved for reference by potential investors, stockholders, the general public and regulators. This is a significant measure to prevent connected transactions unfair to minority interests. Regulators should specifically require the value to be (open) market value, that is to say, it should not reflect the interests of one or some of the main players (specific buyers, specific sellers).

Market value is the key concept to be introduced in the new standards of assets appraisal in China and is one of the key references that determine the price of an asset transaction. Therefore, if the price of the asset transaction appears obviously different to the market value, the company will be required to make supplementary statements to allow the regulators, investors and the general public to make correct and objective judgment to the soundness and fairness of any activities.

Accordingly, by an appraiser providing independent and professional opinion on the market value of assets, management can be positively influenced, the fairness of transactions can be maintained and corporate governance increased. This can also help to prevent parent or connected companies of listed companies either supplying inflated priced assets to or withdrawing assets cheaply from a listed company.

When instructing appraisal work, ensure that the valuer's approach selected is consistent with the appraisal objective.

In appraisal work for assets reorganization, there are a number of other issues to consider for potential investors relying on PRC valuations.

- reorganization plan—there are various forms of acquisition and restructuring. Asset valuations and the approach of appraisers generally can sometimes reflect the perceived reorganization plan;
- property rights—the appraiser should pay special attention to the property rights of the assets, in particular, of the listed companies before 1997. Some listed companies, where one party became a shareholder by contribution by land, still have equity in forms of land transfer and assignment, so equity has both state share form and corporate share form—in such cases, the appraiser should distinguish correctly during the valuation;
- creditors—sometimes the assets transferred to the company may involve the transfer of liabilities;
- due diligence—special importance should be attached to the completeness, compatibility, function or effectiveness of the assets; the status of the property rights; as well as to the compatibility of the assets with documented income, costs, and revenue;

- identify the assumptions and restrictions for assets valuation—this should be reasonable. Where analysis of the development status of the industry and the company is obviously inconsistent with the actual status, the appraiser should explain in detail;
- choose proper appraisal methods—a number of different methods should be used in order to make a comprehensive analysis and correct mistakes; this is now a legal requirement;
- ensure a normal asset appraisal report and attach importance to information disclosure.

Negotiating Strategy in China

Most companies that do not have extensive experience negotiating in China tend to follow the same negotiation strategy when they seek to acquire Chinese assets as they would with an acquisition of a company in their home country, mistakenly believing that applying a few Chinese customs to their set negotiation practices will suffice.

Businessmen traveling to China to negotiate for the first time must do their homework; it is important to have a basic understanding of the Chinese culture, as 2,000 years of cultural developments have understandably shaped the Chinese mindset, thus influencing their approach to negotiation strategy. Additionally, foreign negotiators must be cognizant how this culture influences Chinese negotiating techniques, as well as what they are attempting to achieve through the implementation of these techniques, and have appropriate counter-strategies.

The two of the major philosophical influences on Chinese culture are:

- Confucianism—this philosophy, founded by Confucius over 2,500 years ago, revolves around different hierarchical relationships in society, emphasizing obedience, loyalty and benevolence as admirable qualities
- Taoism—taoism emphasizes on harmony with nature and the universe. One of its central concept is action through inaction. It revolves around opposites (yin and yang) and stresses finding the way between the two

Both philosophies are concerned with the means rather than the end, the process rather than the goal. This concept is often played out in Chinese negotiations, as the Chinese feel that back and forth haggling helps to create an ideal compromise.

Additionally, the current surrounding sociopolitical and economic environment in China continues to influence the negotiating style. Imperialistic exploitation of China has left an intrinsic wariness of foreigners, as well as a general cynicism towards the rule of law in general. At the same time, in China there exists a high degree of bureaucratic complexity, meaning decision making requires authorization at many levels often resulting in competing interests. Thus both current and historical developments in China have significant impacts on Chinese negotiating practices.

C. Devonshire-Ellis et al. (eds.), *Mergers & Acquisitions in China*, China Briefing,
DOI: 10.1007/978-3-642-14919-1_7, © Asia Briefing Ltd. 2011

1 Pre-negotiation

The Long "Getting to Know You" Stage

This stage in China can last much longer than foreign businesses are accustomed to. It can involve attending long, drawn-out expensive banquets, attending sporting events, home visits, and more, during which everything but business is discussed. Very often these events include rounds of heavy drinking. It may be regarded as rude to turn down the offer of a drink, so one must be prepared to deal with the consequences of drinking large quantities of liquor. Those who are particularly averse to the consumption of alcohol may want to prepare a medical excuse to avoid drinking, as this is an acceptable reason not to drink. However, it is important that non-drinkers still participate in the myriad of toasts that will occur over the meal; it's perfectly acceptable to toast with a soft drink, glass of juice, or mineral water.

Under Chinese culture this preliminary stage is essential. This arises largely from importance that Chinese attach to interpersonal harmony. Until recently, Chinese property rights and contract law were virtually non-existent—and are still inadequate by Western standards. Chinese business people have traditionally relied more on good faith than on tightly drafted deals.

Western negotiators coming to China should be prepared for this lengthy process. It is not only standard practice to take a bit longer to get to know the counterpart on a personal level, but also an important tool to create the trust and interpersonal harmony necessary in achieving a mutually beneficial deal.

Not Showing Their Cards until They've Seen Yours

Chinese negotiators will often feign disinterest in foreign enterprises' offers, which can be disconcerting to foreign enterprises who assumed they were arriving in China to negotiate an imminent deal. The Chinese will often use silence as a negotiating tactic, which their Western counterparts will misinterpret as a break-down in the negotiating process, thus making hasty concessions. Chinese enterprises will also often claim they are in negotiations with competing interested parties, further reinforcing the idea that your business is not as important to them as theirs is to you. All of this is enough to make many foreign businessmen either throw their hands up in frustration and walk away from the deal or reveal their bottom line too soon in hopes of pushing the deal through in a more timely fashion.

It is important that foreign enterprises looking to move to China understand how the Chinese are thinking when they take such actions. The Chinese are wary of implementing a win–win strategy as they fear the other side will not reciprocate accordingly this desire to implement a win–win strategy. Instead, the fear of being taken advantage of is one explanation why the Chinese are so reluctant to reveal their true requirements early on in the negotiation process.

It's essential that the foreign firm gathers as much information about the local company prior to arrival in China, so it can have as clear a picture as possible of what will motivate the other side. Additionally, it would behoove a foreign enterprise to draft a number of possible deal scenarios, as widening the spectrum of capabilities and interests the foreign enterprise can demonstrate makes it more difficult for the Chinese side to determine what your primary interest is. Furthermore, if the foreign negotiator has performed well in the "getting to know you" stage, he or she should have created a trusting relationship under which the two sides can work together to reveal their true intentions, desires, and capabilities. Again, patience is a virtue in this situation, as moving too fast will rarely result in the best possible outcome.

2 Negotiation

Chinese Strategic Use of Time

Bargaining sessions are long, changes are frequent, and the Chinese strategic use of time in negotiations can be frustrating and, at times, seem even underhanded. Chinese negotiators will also strive to control the pace and use of time in negotiations in several ways:

- they will often seemingly delay proposals until the last available minute, forcing the foreign enterprise to make on-the-spot decisions or return home empty handed
- they will also delay making commitments and request last minute changes or concessions, putting the foreign negotiator in a difficult situation as well
- the Chinese will also seemingly jump from topic to topic in negotiations, never arriving at any agreement on any one point, thus drawing out the negotiation process

This behavior by Chinese negotiators stems from a few different cultural factors. As mentioned above, the Chinese have a deep-seated distrust of foreigners and a fear of being taking advantage of. Lengthening the negotiation process and forcing foreigners to make on-the-spot decisions is one way they can be more sure they are getting a fair deal.

The Chinese also have great pride in their diligence—to the point of endurance. Chinese negotiators will be better prepared than their Western counterparts, and bargaining sessions are longer than in the West. By lengthening the negotiation process and refusing to commit until the last possible moment, Chinese negotiators are demonstrating their extreme degree of diligence and simultaneously ensuring they are getting the best deal possible.

Finally, the Chinese are aware that foreign negotiators have traveled great distances, are probably tired, and are required to return to their home country within a set period of time. It is not beyond the Chinese to use this knowledge to their advantage, attempting to force tired negotiators under a deadline to make unnecessary concessions.

Foreign negotiators can negate this in several ways:

- they should be able to demonstrate their own diligence to the negotiating process by asking many questions in sessions; asking the same questions more than once is acceptable—doing so shows you are dedicated to understanding every aspect of the deal
- the negotiator should also be prepared to talk about all aspects of the deal simultaneously and in an apparent haphazard manner
- negotiators should use time to their advantage by delaying commitments through reference to back home regulations and needs for superior review
- the foreign negotiator must be prepared to return home without having signed a contract, and more importantly, the home office must fully back the negotiator in this

The Chinese are very good at using time to their advantage in negotiations. Exhibiting diligence, commitment, and a willingness to go home without having completed a goal will not go unnoticed by Chinese business, and will improve the chances of concluding a successful deal.

Creative Use of Information

Chinese negotiators have often been accused of being dishonest in their presentation of information. They may refer to real or fictional regulations, policies, or budget limitations in order to extract concessions from the other side. They may misrepresent their capabilities or willingness to commit to a particular aspect of a deal, only revealing the true situation at a later date, much to the dismay of their foreign counterparts.

To the Chinese, the creative use of information in negotiations is an acceptable strategy. China has only recently begun the arduous process of implementing a legal system that works based upon fixed laws and regulations rather than the previous, more flexible system under which the Chinese Communist Party decided what was acceptable and unacceptable in society, with frequent changes depending upon the political and social mood. Hence, to most Chinese, laws exist in name only; practice can differ vastly. If nobody says it's wrong or stops you from doing it, it must be ok.

In any case, foreign negotiators must be aware of this tendency, and be prepared to combat the tactic accordingly. Should the Chinese apply pressure to negotiate quickly using local policies and regulations, foreign negotiators should likewise use the policies and regulations of their own company to counterbalance this pressure. Most importantly, the foreign negotiator should rely on an intermediary to clarify points of contention. It is foolish to assume that foreign negotiators will be able to identify every situation under which Chinese negotiators are misrepresenting information—a Chinese intermediary is much more apt and well suited for such a task.

Referral of Decision Making to Higher Authorities

Chinese negotiators will frequently reference a need to consult with their superiors on important decisions. This requires frequent breaks from the negotiating process so that the negotiator can confer with his or her superior, and maintain their input. This can cause foreign negotiators to feel discomfort, as they typically operate on the assumption that time is money and frequently misinterpret the Chinese breaks as signs of confusion or insincerity.

During the frequent political purges of the late 20th century in China, it was always decision makers and people that stood by their opinions that suffered the most, those who stayed on the sidelines had a much better chance of going unnoticed and unpunished. Furthermore, the Chinese social system itself is set up as a complex bureaucracy—even something as simple as purchasing a television in a department store requires interaction with a minimum of three different employees with different functions. Hence the Chinese's unwillingness to make independent decisions and need to frequently confer with superiors. Hence, many Chinese are risk averse. They frequently confer with superiors so that they can remain under the radar and avoid making decisions that later might leave them vulnerable to criticism.

Foreign negotiators should accordingly plan for negotiations with frequent breaks to give their Chinese counterparts the time necessary to make such consultations. Foreign negotiators can likewise use this tactic to their advantage, claiming a need to consult with superiors when they are unwilling to immediately make concessions.

It should also be noted that it is important that the foreign country send a negotiator of the appropriate status within the company. Sending a negotiator that is deemed to be inexperienced or of a low position is seen as an insult by the Chinese, and the deal may be doomed before negotiations even start. Eventually there may be a need for higher level members of each organization to meet. However, top-level Chinese executives will not be prepared to bargain, and will not be persuaded. It's simply not their role. As mentioned above, they are there to consult with lower-level negotiators, who in turn play the role of bargainer. Rather, they will evaluate the relationship during a show of sincerity by their Western counterparts.

3 Post-negotiation

Changing Elements of the Contract That Have Already Been Agreed upon

Once negotiations are concluded, Western negotiators may mistakenly believe that a deal has been arrived upon. They are then frustrated and confused by a sudden and unexpected request by the Chinese side to make a change in the contract regarding an issue that had already been discussed in depth and agreed upon. It is also possible that the Chinese will make no indication that they want to make a change, and will present a contract that is ostensibly the same as what had been discussed in negotiations, but in fact represents a changed agreement. Though at times infuriating, the foreign negotiator must expect such requests, and be prepared.

Again, this stems from the Chinese belief that the longer the process of negotiation takes, the better the outcome. To them, re-negotiating after an agreement has been arrived upon is simply a necessary part of ensuring the best possible result. Furthermore this is in line with the Chinese idea that agreements simply represent the beginning of ongoing negotiations.

Foreign negotiators must be prepared to re-negotiate after deals have been arrived upon. However, it is also important for the foreign negotiator to understand that it is better to walk away from the business than to carry it out under unfavorable terms. Such a stance can result in a reputation of tenacity and persistence for the foreign negotiator that is valued by Chinese. The foreign negotiator must keep sight of their bottom line on core issues of the contract and be prepared to refuse to budge beyond that bottom line.

Other Key Points

Beyond understanding the negotiation tactics implemented by Chinese negotiators that have historically aggravated and confused their Western counterparts, there are a few more things about Chinese culture that all foreign businessmen in China should be aware of.

Guanxi

The literal translation for the word is "relationships," but the concept is much broader. It is suffice to say here that in the Chinese business world, guanxi is understood as the network of relationships among various parties that cooperate together and support one another. In competitive business settings in China, more often than not, whoever has the most guanxi comes out on top.

One aspect of guanxi that should never be overlooked is that it revolves around the idea of reciprocity. Maintaining good guanxi requires favors in return of favors. Those who do not reciprocate will not maintain their guanxi, and will be labeled as one who forgets their obligations, and the guanxi will cease to exist. At the same time, this reciprocity is not immediate, but favors should always be remembered and returned. This long-term reciprocity is a cornerstone of enduring personal relationships.

Face

The Chinese attach a much greater level of importance to saving face and giving face than in the West. If Westerners cause the Chinese embarrassment or loss of composure, even unintentionally, it can be disastrous for business negotiations. When those negotiating with the Chinese break promises or display anger, frustration, or aggression at the negotiation table, it results in a mutual loss of face. Causing the Chinese business partner who brought you to the table to lose face is no mere faux pas; it's a disaster.

Thus it is important to ensure that the Chinese do not lose face during negotiations, and equally as important to give face when called for. Westerners cannot possibly be expected to understand all of the different situations pertaining to face, which is why the intermediary (discussed above) is an essential component of successful negotiations.

Language Choice

Some foreigners coming to China who have an extensive background in Mandarin Chinese may feel tempted to utilize their language skills in the negotiations. While speaking Chinese in more informal settings such as the "getting to know you stage" may be acceptable and result in some comical misunderstandings, it is not advised that Western negotiators use Chinese at the negotiating table. Use your native language and a translator, as it is better for a number of reasons.

The Chinese language is complex, and while words in Chinese may have the same literal meaning as in English, the subtler meanings and connotations may differ greatly.

This may lead to misunderstandings where both sides are agreeing, but have different understanding of what they are agreeing to. Furthermore, not speaking Chinese at the negotiation table will make Chinese negotiators feel freer to discuss amongst themselves in Chinese, giving Western Chinese-speakers the opportunity to listen in on their discussion unbeknownst to the other side. You can be sure when you are discussing in English someone from their side of the table is listening in on your conversations, you might as well use the same technique to your advantage as well.

4 Conclusion

Negotiating in China shall remain a difficult task for foreigners, as cultural differences continue to complicate all aspects of the process. It should also be remembered that these cultural differences frustrate not only foreign negotiators, but Chinese negotiators as well, as they too struggle to formulate negotiation strategies that they feel will work best given the cultural differences at hand. At the end of the day, both sides can feel discouraged with a feeling of shaken competence.

Patience, then, is an indispensable quality of foreign negotiators hoping to be successful in China. However backwards the Chinese negotiating process may seem, it is important to understand that the techniques and mindset brought to the negotiating table are the result of a long history of cultural, economic, and political influences. Having a basic knowledge of these influences will help Western negotiators better understand the situation they are facing and come up with appropriate counter-strategies.

Though the negotiation process can be difficult, it is still possible to be successful, as evidenced by the large number of smart Western bargainers who have managed to enjoy great profits in their endeavors in China. Becoming accustomed to the negotiation process in China is neither easy nor instantaneous, but with the right attitude and preparation, successful and mutually beneficial negotiations are possible.

Buying Bankrupt Assets

1 Acquisition of Bankrupt SOEs Assets at Auction

Public Bidding and Auction

Although you may well have first right of refusal, the acquisition of SOEs must now go through a public auction. Essentially, however, the 'public auction' is far from internationally public. An advertisement, in Chinese, is placed in the local paper with details of invitations to bid. The period for submitting bids is usually 20 days, and if no other bid is received, the price for the assets is deemed to be that based upon the final valuation agreement between the two parties submitted to the SASAC/Asset Exchange Centre as mentioned above. If another bid is received, if you possess right of first refusal, you may raise your offer. Obviously the Commission will want to attract the highest bid. In practice however rival bids have thus far been relatively uncommon.

Some practical issues:

1. To buy assets of a domestic enterprise, a foreign investor usually needs to buy through an auction and needs to pay a certain amount of deposit in advance. The reason is that the Chinese government is trying to avoid fraud, and improve bankruptcy reforms. Therefore, as a foreign investor, understanding the target enterprise, as well as the nature of the competing bidders is very important, and will be key success factors for the foreign investor to win the bid.
2. Carefully read the public notice for the bid and completely understand the bidding target, scope of property use, and any extra compensation fees for canceling any purchase contract MOU for the target domestic enterprise.
3. Obtaining favorable tax policies is another important consideration for most foreign investors. In addition, various local tax policies, especially in Western regions, may be available, so explore these thoroughly. If you do not ask, you would not necessarily get these.

C. Devonshire-Ellis et al. (eds.), *Mergers & Acquisitions in China*, China Briefing, DOI: 10.1007/978-3-642-14919-1_8, © Asia Briefing Ltd. 2011

4. Careful drafting of the purchase agreement is another essential discipline of the asset acquisition. In the purchase agreement you need to clarify the following points:

- scope of the property purchased, including the granted land use rights, plant, machinery and the entire establishment
- terms of property purchased, usually 40 years or more according to the negotiation between the two parties
- payment arrangement and payment conditions. It is possible to arrange installment payments. In some cases, it has been possible to pay only 15% of the total price for the first installment after the Chinese party agreed to consign the object of the bid in the auction
- do not forget the clause in the agreement that the Chinese party has the responsibility to liaise with the local government body and tax authorities to enjoy all favorable policies as a wholly foreign owned company—but follow these through yourself as well
- obligations for Parties A and B.

Usually the Chinese party will restrict the foreign investor to using the purchased property for other use rather than the previously agreed purpose. Try to agree on a wider scope for property usage. Additionally, in the payment arrangement clause, try to set a condition like "Party A shall help Party B in finalizing all the business registration procedures before Party B makes the first payment." In addition, clarifying the notice time for certain circumstantial changes, especially timeframes, is also very important, and can avoid conflicts afterwards.

1. *Usually a temporary liquidation committee or a receivership committee will*, on behalf of the target domestic company, negotiate the purchase agreement. If so, do not forget to add a very important term: "Due to the temporary nature of Party A, Party A shall appoint an alternative entity which will take over remaining responsibilities in the event Party A has to withdraw."
2. *Conducting a due diligence review is essential.* The records on many aspects of a Chinese business, such as legal title to land-use rights, the existence of pending litigation, and priority security interests over assets, are often either unavailable or unreliable. Corporate accounting is also frequently lax by foreign standards. Sometimes Chinese companies, particularly SOEs, are accustomed to rigid secrecy policies and may be uncooperative in disclosing their records. As a result, conducting satisfactory due diligence can be difficult. Under these circumstances, most foreign investors will want comprehensive representations and warranties, indemnities for breach, and security for those indemnities. These arrangements are unfamiliar to many Chinese companies, and obtaining acceptable terms and conditions that incorporate them is often a challenge.
3. *Financing.* Numerous obstacles complicate debt financing for M&A transactions. FIEs are most often the acquisition vehicle but are subject to maximum leverage ratios that cap their borrowing ability. Existing FIEs may have already used up some or all of their authorized borrowing. Because procedures for

pledging equity interests or registering security interests in assets are not fully developed, and because enforcement of such interests is difficult at best, banks are often unwilling to loan funds for acquisitions. Even cash payments can give rise to problems because of the inconvertibility of the RMB. If the Chinese party is required to make the payments in hard currency, it may be unable to obtain SAFE authorization for the conversion. When the foreign party is bringing new funds into China to make the acquisition, it must consider that, once converted to RMB and registered in the FIEs capital account, its funds may be difficult to convert back to hard currency and repatriate later.

4. *Lack of legal holding entity.* Additionally, as is often the case, the asset may only recently become available and the foreign company may have no pertinent legal entity in China to purchase the assets. In this case negotiations with the provincial government and SAFE may allow the auction bid price to be registered via SAFE, and the bid at auction will be specifically identified as only being valid if the bid is permitted to be shown as registered capital for a new WFOE. After the auction takes place, monies will be transferred prior to the WFOE being incorporated, and both the assets and the purchase price will be later permitted to be shown as registered capital for the new WFOE when its licensing procedures are completed.

5. *Taxes.* Profits derived from the sale of an investment in an FIE or Chinese domestic company are taxable income; a withholding tax of 10% applies if the seller is an off shore company; and transfers among affiliated enterprises may not be taxable events but may require adjustments in the cost basis for the investment. Many other complex tax and accounting issues may arise, and should be checked.

Typical acquisitions take about 6 months to achieve with the following deliverables:

(1) Identification, valuation and due diligence of assets.
(2) Due diligence on the liquidation committee and understanding of the unformed WFOE (obtained via SAFE).
(3) Auction bid and purchase contract.
(4) Transfer of funds to SAFE account.
(5) Establishment of the WFOE.
(6) Transfer of all assets and asset purchase fee to the WFOE.
(7) Normal WFOE operational administration procedures completed.
(8) Plant and assets operational.

Additional Information

- The Chinese government has already allowed foreign investors to directly purchase SOEs, which gives foreign investors a greater chance to purchase valuable assets at low prices, but "reasonable asset evaluation" is the key phrase

- Management Buy Out (MBOs) have become the most popular method to reform SOEs in China, which also give foreign investors opportunities to take part in the campaign. However, handling the burden of dismissed employees and being subject to their welfare payments are still major hurdles to overcome

A foreign investor can not only be a purchaser for the assets or equity of a domestic company, but can also be a fund provider (financing group); this is because the MBO makes most Chinese senior management staff require additional capital to buy shares of the target company and usually they are short of this due to having had a low level salary history.

- Northeast China and Northwest China are great target areas for foreign investors; the government has announced policies to develop these regions, and offer favorable policies regarding taxation incentives

Different Basic M&A Mechanisms in Use at Present

LBO: Leveraged Buy Out

It is a traditional way to purchase a target company. Its characteristics are to try to buy more assets by using less as capital. Usually using LBO requires the investor to use assets of the target company as a guarantee to borrow initial investment capital from banks or other financing groups, therefore, the investor should pay more attention to the cash inflows of the resulting entity in order to pay up the debt as soon as possible. Profitability and payback periods are the most important considerations for LBO.

MBO: Management Buy Out

These are becoming more popular in China. This is because the Chinese government has been conducting a reform of SOEs. The purpose is to release the government from the financing of these and to foster an entrepreneurial economy. The Chinese government has recently modified the National Constitution and for the first time admits and accepts private economists, which will facilitate MBO processes significantly in China. By using MBO, a foreign investor can try to encourage existing Chinese senior management staff to take part in leveraged buyouts. Therefore, if as a foreign investor, you need local management staff and want to reduce agency fees, you can choose MBO. Be aware however that MBOs are not suitable for a listed company.

IPO: Initial Public Offering

Similar to venture capital, it is a strategic investment. The characteristics of IPO are that the investor wants to list the resulting entity in the stock exchange after acquiring, business reengineering and integrating. The way to make profit is by issuing the initial stock.

Employee Stock Ownership Plan (ESOP) and Employee Buy Out (EBO)

These are characterized by allowing the employees to buy the shares. In these models, the staff have dual status, as both employee and owner. ESOP and EBO are better suited for Chinese-only SOEs.

2 Conclusion

China's FDI environment has significantly improved and foreign investors now stand a greater chance of entering the Chinese market via acquisition rather than to go greenfield. To ensure the success of the new business, an in depth understanding of Chinese relevant rules, regulations and business cultural difference are key factors. To achieve this, working with an experienced M&A consultant in China is a must.

Labor Issues in M&A

1 Introduction

China's economy is booming and a more active participation in the global marketplace requires stricter laws and regulations in compliance with world standards for working and employment conditions. However, in spite of existing labor laws, companies still underpay their staff, require them to work for extreme periods of time without rest and ignore health and safety measures. Many cases in which we have conducted due diligence on companies in China, we have come across non- or under-payment of wages or social welfare. This can be especially dangerous when acquiring companies or parts of companies as one may also acquire all the liabilities.

Foreign investors have to be in compliance with all the laws and regulations of the PRC—even if local Chinese companies are not. Foreign investors are the number one target of legal and financial control mechanisms in China. Before the Chinese authorities check local companies' compliance issues, they will check the foreign investor. Therefore, a foreign investor has to make sure they are in compliance with China's often changing laws and regulations. If you are not sure that you are in compliance, you are well advised to work with someone who can help. Make sure that your Chinese documents are in compliance with all laws and regulations. You are in China, so only the Chinese version is the binding one.

2 The Labor Law

On June 29, 2007, the Standing Committee of the National People's Congress adopted the Labor Contract Law of the People's Republic of China, which came into effect on January 1, 2008.

C. Devonshire-Ellis et al. (eds.), *Mergers & Acquisitions in China*, China Briefing, DOI: 10.1007/978-3-642-14919-1_9, © Asia Briefing Ltd. 2011

The law applies to all employers within the People's Republic of China. In addition to commercial enterprises, it must be followed by government agencies, public institutions and social organizations. It governs the establishment of employment relationships as well as the performance and termination of employment contracts. The provisions prescribed by the law are meant to discourage employers from signing short-term labor contracts and will have a direct impact on employment costs. The aim of the law is to improve the employment relationship, clarify the rights and obligations of employees and employers and give more stability and security for the employees in the PRC.

The law will considerably change the requirements for both employer and employee and requires many companies, both foreign and domestic, to review their labor contracts.

The labor law is part of the general trend to unify legislation relating to domestic Chinese and foreign invested enterprises, although some people fear that the fast, and to a high degree compliant, implementation of the law by FIEs might lead to disadvantages versus local competitors.

This labor law takes great steps towards protecting the rights of individual workers in China by confirming workers' rights to negotiate their own written employment contract with their employer, specifying terms, conditions and benefits. It also enhances specific individual rights in the arenas of probationary period, health and hygiene standards, layoff compensation, generally making it more difficult for employers to terminate their contracts.

Labor issues play a large role in M&A considerations in China. Carrying out due diligence to understand the target firm's labor situation is essential. The timely payment of wages, contributions to social insurance and housing funds, retirement related issues, and the changing role of labor unions are all areas that purchasing firms need to investigate when attempting M&A with firms in China, as well as understanding the relevant laws and the obligations they will be faced with upon acquisition of the target firm.

After acquiring an enterprise in China, the purchaser must consider if and how to restructure the internal organization of the target acquisition so that it can work best in the context of the acquirer's organizational structure. Chinese firms tend to be vastly overstaffed and downsizing is often a necessity if the target firm is to become successful.

Additionally, the purchasing firm may find the need to reorganize the management's structure and appoint executives that not only are familiar with the purchaser's organization but are also trustworthy and reliable, as well as transferring or laying off previous management. Studies have shown that contrary to intuition, foreigners in upper management positions in Chinese companies may actually perform better than Chinese managers. It has been suggested this arises due to the fact that Chinese upper management is torn between loyalties to their fellow-countrymen and to their employers. Siding with employers can be seen as a betrayal by Chinese workers. Foreign managers, on the other hand, are expected to side with the purchasing company, and doing so does not cause as much unrest among Chinese workers. Thus, it is also mandatory that purchasing investors understand the laws and regulations regarding the layoffs, re-positioning and transfer of employees.

3 Employing Chinese Staff

It may be very useful to have a Chinese employee help you with all aspects of setting up your China operations, including all business licenses, offices, bank accounts, handling all documentation and so on, due to the fact that the language and bureaucracy are almost unintelligible. However, it is not normal business practice—anywhere—to have one person in control of all aspects of your country operations, and with very good reason:

- Their abilities may not stretch as far as international competencies—the way in which foreign companies have to be administered in China, and the reporting structures they have to go through, are very different from those that Chinese companies have to adhere to. In reality, foreign businesses in China face far more scrutiny than Chinese companies do. If your employees, good as they are, are not familiar with the regulatory aspects concerning operating and maintaining an international office or business in China, chances are there will be issues on which your company will immediately be out of compliance. That can, and does, get expensive. Additionally, there are circumstances where an employee may deliberately keep the company out of compliance, to obtain benefits or other leeway later if any argument arises against their favor
- Having one person in control of all your corporate documents and/or banking is very common in China. But the risks are obvious. You can lose all your abilities to operate the company overnight if they decide to walk out of the door. Plus all your money
- Insertion of family and friends into your supply chain is also very common, not just in China. You need to audit your purchasing and sales departments regularly to ensure employees are not placing orders with companies owned by friends or relatives that are then charging your business at rates well over the market odds. Be sure to check any offshore subsidiary the target business has, as this practice is commonly carried out worldwide
- Setting up of parallel business—this involves employees establishing their own mirror company in competition with the employer. There have been cases where such mirror companies have a similar sounding Chinese name to the international brand, and divert all orders to that business instead

4 Employing Expatriate Staff

There are problems with expatriate staff as well:

- Hiring lawyers with no China experience is expensive, and there is not really much point, especially if their Chinese language capabilities are minimal. International lawyers are great at international work—cross border structuring and so on—but far too many of them profess expertise in areas of China practice they are neither qualified nor experienced to be dealing with
- Hiring personnel on their language skills alone—young graduates do have skills of course, but do not weigh them down too much with managerial responsibilities before they have had time to adjust them to a commercial business environment and have found their feet around your business. A management development program designed to maximize on their language skills yet introduce them to your business will reap greater rewards both for you and for them if you treat them with continuing educational attention
- The China guys—expats of note are those who really know their way around, and can steer you away from all the problems we have identified. They will have a good grasp of the language, and may well have settled down with family here

You cannot survive in China without knowing how to get on, and this is a matter of experience as well as possessing inherent patience, tenacity and people and communications skills. They are available—interestingly at this time, many of the established multinationals are localizing and other talent is perhaps more available in China than ever before.

5 Good Recruitment Practice

- This applies to all staff, irrespective of nationality. There is no reason not to incorporate the normal checks and balances that you would back home
- Check language skills both orally and written—some Chinese staff have their friends write their English CVs for them, while many expatriates overstate the fluency of their Chinese. Note also that regional dialects can enhance or limit the ability of your staff to operate locally.
- Check all backgrounds and references—this is often neglected, and often regretted later. Follow up those qualifications and references. You are paying for them so make sure they are really part of the package
- Pay staff properly—if you want to retain them, pay them properly. Not just their welfare payments that you should be making in any event, but enough to keep them motivated and keen on continuing to work for you. China may be the current centre of cheap manufacturing—but there is no reason for you to be cheap when it comes to your staff. Or you will end up spending more time on recruitment operations than on your actual money-making operations

6 Wage Payment

Employees must be paid on a monthly basis—failure to do so over a prolonged period of time will result in the accrual of large balances. Legal due diligence with regard to the target company's salary payment records including overtime payment should be made in advance to avoid taking over large debts.

7 Social Insurances and Housing Fund

Chinese labor law also requires employers to make monthly contributions to what is referred to as the "Five Insurances and One Fund" which encompasses retirement, medical, unemployment, work-related injury and birth insurance along with a housing fund. Additionally the employer is responsible for paying employees' social security premiums. Should the target company fall behind on any of these payments (which often occurs due to lax enforcement) the purchasing company faces the danger of being exposed to legal liabilities arising from failed insurance and fund contributions.

8 Retirement Related Issues

Enterprises, especially state-owned enterprises, may be responsible for providing retirees a pension in addition to other benefits. Thus, careful due diligence must be carried out on any existing contracts or appropriate agreements.

9 Labor Unions

- The role of labor unions has been strengthened. The current laws, which require employers to notify labor unions prior to terminating a labor contract for any reason, are still in effect. Employers that do not have established labor unions are required to notify the union at the next higher level. Unions are also allowed to engage in collective bargaining and enter into collective contracts
- A company is required to gain approval for its employee manuals, and company rules require a consultation with the labor union, workers' congress, or by workers' representative assembly or equal negotiation, before implementation

82 Labor Issues in M&A

- If the labor union or an employee is of the opinion that the rule or regulation is inappropriate then it should be improved after consultation
- The labor bureau has the right to order an employer to change company rules that violate laws and administrative statues

The purchasing company needs to investigate whether a labor union is established in the target company and for how long is its duration. If so, then the acquiring company must pay 2% of the total salary of all employees to the union and provide the union with office space.

Additionally, the purchasing company needs to research the existence of collective contracts which are concluded between the labor union and the employer. The law also makes allowances for region-wide and industry-wide collective contracts within regions with salary standards lower than the county level. Due diligence is imperative otherwise firms may find themselves entered into legally binding collective contracts whose existence they were previously unaware of.

Labor unions must also be consulted when firms change policy regarding wages, working hours, vacation time, labor safety and hygiene, insurance and other benefits, training, and other related issues. Additionally, labor unions are to be consulted in the case that firms institute large-scale layoffs. Thus it can be seen that it is important for foreign investors to research and understand the situation regarding labor unions in their target firms.

10 Layoffs

In the case of mergers or divisions of an employer, original employment contracts shall continue to be valid, and continue to be performed by the employer which inherits its rights and obligations. Should lay-offs become necessary following M&A transactions, it is imperative that employers fully grasp the Labor Contract Law so that they can legally and efficiently re-organize the workforce.

11 Layoffs Following Acquisition of Equity Interest

The Labor Contract Law allows for employment relationships to be terminated upon mutual consent. According to article 39 of the law, an employer may also terminate an employment contract without the generally accepted 30 days prior notice under any of the following conditions:

- during the probation period the worker proves not to be suited to the employment conditions
- the employee seriously violates the employer's regulations
- the employee seriously neglects their duty, practices graft, or causes serious injury to the employer

11 Layoffs Following Acquisition of Equity Interest

- the employee simultaneously establishes an employment relationship with another employer, which has a serious influence on their ability to perform their tasks for the first employer, or after the employer's objection, the employee refuses to make the necessary changes
- the employee uses deceitful and forceful methods or takes advantage of the employers difficulties to cause the employer to conclude or modify an employment contract that is contrary to the employer's true intent
- the employee is under investigation for committing a crime

While it is possible there are wide scale instances of some of these occurring, it is unlikely that an employer would be able to use the circumstances in article 39 to effectively implement the necessary layoffs that arise following acquisition of an enterprise.

Article 40 of the Labor Contract Law also makes provisions under which employment contracts may be terminated, given that the employer gives the employee 30 days notice or 1 month's pay

- the employee falls ill or suffers a non-work related injury, the legal recovery period has expired, and the worker is unable to continue work as before, and the employer is unable to make separate arrangements for the employee to work
- the employee is unable to perform their duties even after receiving the necessary training or being reassigned to another post
- a major change in the objective circumstances relied upon at the time of conclusion of the employment contract renders it un-performable and, after consultations, the employer and worker are unable to reach an agreement on amending the employment contract

Article 41 outlines the conditions under which an employer may implement large-scale layoffs, defined as the dismissal of 20 employees or 10% of the staff, whichever is larger. The employer is required to announce the layoffs 30 days prior to termination of the employment contracts. Furthermore, the employer is required to "consult" with the relevant labor union and hear their opinions, as well as reporting the planned personnel reduction to the labor administration authority. This language has been watered down from a previous version of the law which gave labor unions veto power over large-scale layoffs. The conditions under which large-scale layoffs may be implemented are as follows:

- the company is making necessary restructuring in accordance with enterprise bankruptcy law
- the production process is undergoing serious difficulties
- the enterprise is changing products/production, experiencing great technical innovation or management style adjustment, and after adjusting employment contracts, personnel reduction is still required
- another major change in the objective circumstances relied upon at the time of conclusion of the employment contracts, rendering them un-performable

The need to restructure an enterprise's workforce as a result of an M&A transaction does in principle qualify as a "major change in the objective circumstances," as set out in item 4 of article 41. It could also be argued that M&A transactions can result in management style adjustment.

The article also outlines which employees shall be given job security priority when employers implement layoffs. Employers shall give priority to keeping on the following workers:

- workers that have signed relatively long-term fixed contracts
- workers that have signed open-term contracts
- households that have no other workers, and need to support the elderly or children

Furthermore, article 42 of the law expressly prohibits the layoff of workers pursuant to articles 40 and 41 of the law if "the worker has worked continuously for 15 years and has less than 5 years until legal retirement age" or is "pregnant, in the pre/post pregnancy stages, or nursing."

Finally, should an enterprise look to re-hire employees within 6 months of layoffs, it shall give priority to re-hiring employees who have been previously laid off.

Article 41 in the Labor Contract Law will be the article that employers rely upon when implementing layoffs as a result of M&A of equity interest transactions. It follows that employers should pay attention to and adhere to the relevant requirements on time frames, reporting and layoff priorities.

12 Layoffs Following Asset Deals

Asset deals do not involve the automatic transfer of employees, therefore, the restructuring of the target's workforce should not be an issue for the purchaser. However, when a foreign investor acquires a domestic target by share or asset deal amongst others, it is necessary to submit an "arrangement" for the employees of the domestic target enterprise to the relevant approval authority. Upon acquisition of FIEs the same conditions will apply.

13 Severance Pay

If employment contracts have been terminated according to articles 38, 40, or 41 of the Labor Contract Law, the employer is required to provide dismissed workers with severance pay. Generally speaking the amount to be paid shall be equivalent to one month's salary for each year of service. Severance pay shall not exceed 12 months' salary. Furthermore, the calculated 1 month's salary shall not exceed three times the official average monthly salary (published annually by the local government) for the region in which the enterprise is located.

14 Re-positioning of Employees

Upon consent of the relevant employees, investors may amend the content of the labor contract, which would include amendment of duties, ranks or powers. The employer also has the right to terminate an employment contract provided they give 30 days notice, and if "the employee is unable to perform their duties even after receiving the necessary training or being reassigned to another post." Other laws contain no further provisions regarding the reassignment of employee's positions or responsibilities.

15 Transfer of Employees

In the case of asset deals, acquiring companies may find the need to transfer employees from the target company to an FIE that was created to acquire the said assets. This will require the termination of contracts with the target company and conclusion of new contracts with the FIE. The above mentioned regulations on termination of employment contracts and severance payments will still apply in this instance. The purchasing company should give adequate consideration to the legal and financial implications of such a transfer.

16 Unresolved Issues

One of the main problems with labor laws in China is their enforcement. The central government drafts, passes, executes and enforces the law—there is no division of power on the mainland. That means a system of checks and balances found in most developed countries does not exist in China. Many companies from Europe and the USA complain that labor laws in China are weakly enforced against Chinese entities, which frequently evade or ignore the law, whereas USA and European companies are monitored very closely. This is not only a burden, but also a chance to create a fair and humane working environment for millions of workers employed directly by FIEs, or as part of the supply chain the company overlooks. It remains questionable how local companies will respond and how provincial jurisdictions will interpret the law. Like any new law in China, there is plenty of room for broad interpretations and the main problem with it, as well as other existing laws remains, and that is the utter vagueness of them.

17 Implications of the Labor Contract Law for Foreign-Invested Entities

The ultimate consequence of the new labor law will be the effective abolition of fixed-term contracts. Every fixed-term contract that expires creates a severance obligation. Business costs will rise due to the higher expenses for hiring and terminating staff. Increasing obligations and legal requirements lead to declining employment flexibility and rising employment risk. However, those who have intently followed the previous drafts will notice that the cost increases could have been even higher. Companies will need to reassess their China HR capability and decide if someone should be designated to handle labor issues, if they do not have an established department. Possible solutions could be outsourcing or part-time employment. In all cases you should act with caution, especially when drafting contracts and company policies. Consider hiring a professional advisor to make sure contracts are in compliance with the new law and to avoid unnecessary administration and legal costs due to incomplete or worse, invalid contracts.

Besides drafting the contracts and revising the pay structures, companies can also be proactively involved in the process of establishing an employee representation committee (ERC) or unions in order to build a strong and trusting communication basis. As collective bargaining will be reinforced, a good relationship with the ERC/union advances cooperation and may help to influence their decisions. The Labor Contract Law improves the power of unions and serves to better inform employees of their rights, which might encourage workers to do more to enforce better working conditions. The law is aimed at changing unfair labor practices that are not employed by most foreign companies (e.g. confiscating employee ID cards or collecting a security payment to detain them is common practice in Chinese entities).

Employers should...

- make themselves familiar with the Labor Contract Law;
- prepare basic contracts for new employees that meet the legal requirements (in Chinese);
- prepare or revise employee handbooks;
- review existing contracts and pay structures (open or fixed-tem, non-compete/ confidentiality clauses, probation period arrangements);
- update or draft company rules;
- establish an employee register and draft a termination certificate;
- review cost impact and create annual provisions (severance, compensation);
- have HR connect with the union/worker representation (expect collective bargaining, and involvement in policy decisions);
- plan for increased labor costs in the near future;
- review staffing agency arrangements (check for outsourcing options).

Tax Planning in M&A

1 General

Tax planning is a vital element during the pre-deal phase of an M&A. However, regulations relating to M&A in China lack coherence and are quite inconsistent. There exist a number of rules and regulations which supplement the general tax laws and regulations. Some of the more important issues to consider are as follows.

2 Registration With the Tax Authorities

This must be done within 30 days of registering with the competent AIC regardless of whether you are establishing a new FIE, merging with other enterprises, terminating or changing your registration details.

3 Share Deals/Equity Acquisition

- Foreign investors who sell equity interest are subject to a tax rate of 10% on profits
- Any losses incurred from the sale of equity interest can in principle be made up by the seller provided that the sale was conducted at a fair price
- Pre-acquisition losses of a domestic enterprises may be carried forward by the newly established FIE and made up to the extent that they have not been used yet

C. Devonshire-Ellis et al. (eds.), *Mergers & Acquisitions in China*, China Briefing, DOI: 10.1007/978-3-642-14919-1_10, © Asia Briefing Ltd. 2011

- All equity interest held by foreign investors is transferred to Chinese parties when the FIE is converted to a domestic enterprise
- Will be liable for Corporate Income Tax (generally 25%, if the vendor is a domestic company) or Withholding Tax (generally 10%, if the vendor is a foreign enterprise)
- Both vendor and purchaser are subject to stamp duty tax of 0.05%, except for the subscription of shares newly issued by the stock limited company
- If an FIE reinvests profits by using capital to establish further FIEs, providing they operate for no less than 5 years, then the FIE may be refunded 40% of the income tax already paid on the reinvested amount; however, this is not applicable to the foreign investor if the FIEs reinvested profits are generated prior to the acquisition

4 Asset Acquisition

- All gains or losses on transfer of assets will be included in the taxable income of the target company
- Providing that the transferor and transferee do not change their production or business operations following the asset transfer, any preferential tax treatment previously enjoyed, may be continued
- Operating losses incurred by the parties of an asset transfer may in principle not be transferable from one to another
- Business tax is applicable for the sales of real properties and intangible assets
- VAT is applicable to the purchaser for sales of equipment, machinery and inventories and is subject to the deduction of input tax
- Internally disposing of assets means that no income is recognized and the historical costs of the relevant shall continue to acrue
- Deed tax is imposed on the purchaser for any real estate, asset sale and purchase contract and is subject to stamp tax

5 Mergers

- Exemption from taxation of capital gains; assets, liabilities and shareholder's equity interest will be transferred to the newly established company
- Revaluation of assets or adjustments to book values during the merger may take place but shall not affect the income tax payable or create amortization gains
- Tax holidays and reductions shall not be repatriated
- Losses incurred by the merger parties must be recorded in the books of the post-merger entity based on their historical book value
- Tax obligations and losses may be taken over by the post-merger party

5 Mergers

- Pro-rata swap of equity interest in one of the merger parties against equity interest in the post-merger entity will not be regarded as a sale and purchase of equity interest

6 Tax and Finance

Tax is never a popular subject wherever you do business, but it is unavoidable. Every foreign investor needs to be aware of what taxes they are liable for, how to calculate those liabilities, and when you can claim exemptions.

This chapter includes details on Corporate Income Tax as well as the much misunderstood financial issue of registered capital and its impact on the application for WFOE and foreign invested commercial enterprises (FICE). For more detailed information about taxes in China, please refer to China Briefing's The China Tax Guide.

7 Registered Capital Calculations

Correctly Calculating Your Total and Registered Capital Requirements

As was explained in detail in Chapter Titled "Chinese Legislation on M&A", mistakes when calculating your registered capital requirements are unfortunately rather common in China, not least due to the misused and misunderstood term "Minimum Registered Capital" as a qualifying statement of necessary financing. You must capitalize your business properly. Much of this can be gleaned from a pragmatic approach to correctly calculating your business start up costs and operational cash-flow requirements and these should be identified in your business plan. Registered capital is required to the amount that is necessary to fund the business until it can break even on its own accord. Re-financing it if you run out is a complicated procedure and requires official approval and assistance from the State Administration of Foreign Exchange to identify additional funding as for registered capital purposes. If these procedures are not followed, any money sent to the business to make up any operational shortfall will be regarded as taxable income. There are other financial requirements that are often overlooked when working out your necessary capitalization, especially with planning for post-registration customs duties and registration requirements.

The financial aspects of these are often also misunderstood or misrepresented, and if not catered for can create serious cash-flow problems almost immediately after incorporation and the commencement of your business operations. We identify these as follows.

Important Tax and Start Up Funding Issues

VAT Treatment

There is still one common misconception about "VAT Exemption on Exports". If the refund rate is lower than the levied rate, the company must bear the additional VAT cost on exportation. The VAT cost is calculated as follows.
Manufacturing company:

VAT cost = (export − imported duty free raw materials excluding customs duty)
× (levy rate − refund rate)

Trading company:

VAT cost = (the cost of local purchased raw material)
× (levy rate − refund rate)

Generally speaking, the levied rate is 17 percent, the refunded rate is based on the goods and can vary from 0 to 17 percent, although there have been some changes recently for low-tech products and those whose production process uses large amounts of energy. Get your professional advisors to check the most up-to-date position.

You need to ensure, if you fall into this scenario, that you have sufficient registered capital to hand to fund this cash-flow gap.

Customs Duties on Imported Raw Materials to be Subsequently Exported

We often hear the misconceived statement, "there is no VAT and Custom Duty levied on imported raw materials used for manufacturing goods locally if these are then finally exported 100 percent". It is incorrect. Actually, newly established Foreign Invested Enterprises must still make a tax deposit to customs for VAT (at around 17 percent) and remit duty on the initial importation, generally for 6 months. Many new businesses do not budget for this as initial working capital to be contributed as part of registered capital, leaving them short of cash later. You must factor this amount based upon your participated imports into your registered capital requirements when working out your required capital injection and cash flow forecasts. It is a common mistake and can have very serious implications if it is not catered for at your financial planning stage.

Other Government Departments that Require Attention

Factories, health and safety and the fire department will all require checks and be responsible for issuing their own licenses, for which you will have to pay. These

7 Registered Capital Calculations

are usually minimal amounts, but can add up for sizable businesses. Environmental protection can however be expensive—if your business is potentially polluting, you need to be aware beforehand how this matter needs to be dealt with and the likely costs for dealing with it. All this needs to be catered for—yes, as your working capital, as reflected in your registered capital injection for operating costs.

General VAT Payer Status

You also need to consider whether your company needs to apply for "General VAT Payer" status. The benefit of having General VAT Payer status is that it gives the VAT payer the right to issue VAT receipts to their clients, which allows them to deduct the input VAT from purchases when it pays output VAT for sales, as well as getting a VAT refund.

For the FICEs or WFOEs who deal with clients that need to issue VAT receipts such as for industrial related produces, they will normally require VAT General Tax Payer status, but if the FICE is only engaged in trading consumable products to individual customers, then this will probably not be necessary.

The requirements for obtaining General VAT Payer status are as follows:

- for manufacturing WFOEs, the annual sales revenue must be up to RMB1 million; in some cities the tax bureau may accept the sales contracts totaling up to RMB1 million as revenue supporting the approval of the general tax payer qualification
- for FICEs, when any of the below conditions qualify, the company can be approved as the general tax payer

  - the company must have annual sales in excess of RMB1.8 million
  - the registered capital shall be at least RMB5 million and the total number of employees shall be over 50 (this can be negotiable in some cities)

Again, this is an issue that will have an impact on the level of registered capital you need in order to begin operations.

8 Total investment Capital

The difference between registered capital and total investment represents the debt of the investment and can be made up by loans from the investor or foreign banks. Pay attention to the relationship between registered capital and total investment in case you need to obtain further debt or other financing from your holding company or other financial institution. Keeping this window open will cost you nothing, but closing yourself off from further financing by equating registered capital and total investment may leave you handcuffed. The payment schedule of the WFOE registered capital also needs to be specified in the Articles of Association. The investor may choose to pay it as a lump sum or in installments.

Please see the table for the required ratios between registered capital and total investment capital.

Total investment (USD)	Registered capital (Min.)
3 million or below	7/10 of the total investment
Above 3 million and under 4.2 million	2.1 million
4.2 million to 10 million	1/2 of the total investment
Above 10 million and under 12.5 million	5 million
12.5 million to 30 million	2/5 of the total investment
Above 30 million and under 36 million	12 million
36 million or above	1/3 of the total investment

Notes: (1) If it is stipulated in the contract or Articles of Association that the registered capital shall be contributed in one lump sum, all investors shall contribute all subscribed investment within 6 months after the business license is issued. (2) If it is stipulated in the contract or Articles of Association that the registered capital shall be paid in instalments, all investors shall contribute at least 20 percent of its subscribed investment in the first instalment and shall be paid within 3 months after the business license is issued.

9 Business Taxes

The State Administration of Taxation (SAT) is the body in charge of tax administration in China—the equivalent of the IRS in the USA or the Inland Revenue in the UK. It drafts legislation, sets collection targets and collects revenue itself, via the regional State Tax Bureau. The Ministry of Finance also issues circulars affecting tax from time to time, but only following approval from the SAT. Tax incomes go to two different pools in China—the State Tax Bureau, which funds central government, and the local tax bureau, which funds local government. Each business entity has to register with both state and local bureaus, and has to pay different taxes to each. In addition, be aware that many tax regulations are subject to interpretation by tax officials, and the same regulation may thus be implemented in different ways in different parts of the same city.

The SAT website is at www.chinatax.gov.cn—some SAT regulations are also published on the MOC site at http://english.mofcom.gov.cn/.

Converting a Chinese Company into an FIE

1 Converting Joint Ventures to WFOEs

Given that no new foreign investor is being introduced, converting an existing JV to a WFOE is essentially a re-approval procedure that is reasonably straightforward to accomplish. However, the following must be taken into consideration beforehand:

- Is the industry that you are in a non-restricted activity that does not require a Chinese partner?
- Is the mechanism for purchase or transfer of shares adequately catered for in the JV articles?

Valuation of Shares and Assets

Point 1 is a review of the articles and a look at the mechanism for transfer. This may involve a valuation of the business, in which case both parties need to agree on this. Local valuation firms may not be entirely impartial. If you can, insist upon an independent valuer with international experience. Ideally, the preferred list of valuers should have been specified in the articles from the outset. Often there are no such articles and a board resolution to appoint a specific firm may need to be negotiated and passed.

Board Resolutions

Assuming that a price has been agreed, further unanimous board resolutions need to be passed before converting the JV to a WFOE. Usually these will tie in with an agreement over transfer of capital to purchase the equity, which then triggers the share transfer.

Re-approval

This accomplished, it is a relatively straightforward process of submitting a new set of Articles of Association, application letter and the equity transfer contract, etc., to the original examining and approving authority (whichever local govern-

C. Devonshire-Ellis et al. (eds.), *Mergers & Acquisitions in China*, China Briefing, DOI: 10.1007/978-3-642-14919-1_11, © Asia Briefing Ltd. 2011

ment approved the original JV) or the competent examining and approving authority when there is capital increase or business scope expansion, etc. These should include of course reference to the different set of laws that govern the activities of WFOEs, a new board of directors, and possibly other managerial positions as well (see our related book Setting Up Wholly Foreign-Owned Enterprises in China, for more details).

One advantage of converting JVs to WFOEs is that it may not be required to inject any further capital into the business, as the JV will of course have already been essentially capitalized.

Once the new set of documents is filed, the old JV chops and licenses are handed back to the authorities and the new structure is registered as having taken its place. New chops, licenses and other pertinent certificates are issued and away you go. It is possible to keep operations intact and on-going during this process—it is not in anyone's interest for the business to have any down time as this would mean a loss of tax revenues for the local government!

Consolidated Tax Breaks

One area that can prove awkward is if this involves converting multiple JVs in different locations that have been enjoying tax breaks, but which are not in synchronization as regards time span. This will need to be negotiated with the new tax authority in the new location that will require seeing the relevant tax bureau documents from other locations prior to making a decision. Regional tax bureaus are usually fair when it comes to reevaluating multiple tax breaks and consolidating these into one—it just takes a bit of time and patience in explaining the intricacies of the previous holidays. This is an issue you may need to watch with the recent changes to the corporate income tax laws.

Acquiring Staff

Be aware that if you convert to a WFOE, your pension fund or redundancy liabilities are extended back to the time when you first formed the JV—not from day one of the converted WFOE. Have a look at your human resource issues beforehand if acquiring numerous staff—especially if having to make redundancies or planned layoffs later. It can get expensive.

Summary

Most of the problems encountered with conversion are inadequate provisions catering for it in the original articles. These of course can be amended but will need to be done beforehand to allow a smooth transition. A review is a pre-requisite.

2 Liquidating Joint Ventures

The procedures for closing a JV—its dissolution and liquidation—are no easier or shorter than for the process of setting up such a company, and normally take between 6 and 9 months to complete.

2 Liquidating Joint Ventures

According to PRC law, a joint venture may be dissolved in the following situations:

1. Termination of the duration of the venture.
2. Inability to continue operations due to heavy losses.
3. Inability to continue operations due to the failure of one of the contracting parties to fulfill its obligations prescribed in the agreement, contract and articles of association.
4. Inability to continue operations due to heavy losses caused by force majeure.
5. Failure to obtain the desired objectives of the operation and no prospects for future development.
6. Occurrence of other reasons for dissolution as prescribed in the contract and Articles of Association.

Upon the declaration of dissolution, the company is required to start the liquidation procedures.

For the above list 2, 4–6, the board of directors should make an application to the approving authority for approval, while for above list 3, the performing party is entitled to make the application.

Note also that according to the new Company Law, if a JV made a substantial loss in operation, but its Articles of Association do not provide a right to terminate in these circumstances and the shareholders or board cannot reach a unanimous resolution on termination, a minority shareholder with not less than 10% of shares may take legal action to petition for termination. Upon obtaining an order from court, the JV may proceed with liquidation and winding up.

Creation of a Liquidation Committee

1. The board will need to appoint a liquidation committee to handle the liquidation within 15 days from the dissolution date of the company.
2. The liquidation committee shall liquidate and value the company's assets in accordance with the PRC Law and the Articles of Association.
3. The liquidation committee shall consist of at least three members and the members usually should be the directors of the board. However, if the director of the board is not suitable to be the member of the liquidation committee, the liquidation committee may engage certified public accountants and lawyers.
4. The liquidation committee shall have the right to terminate employment contracts, to sell, export, transfer, assign or otherwise dispose of any and all assets belonging to the company whether they be inside or outside the PRC, as well as to conclude all business matters of the Company, in accordance with PRC Law and the principles set out in the Articles of Association.
5. The liquidation committee shall exercise the following functions and powers during liquidation:

   (a) liquidate the assets of the company, prepare a balance sheet and list of assets, and formulate the liquidation plan;

(b) make an announcement for the benefit of unknown creditors and notify known creditors in writing;
(c) complete any unfinished business of the company;
(d) submit the appraisal and valuation of assets and the basis for calculation;
(e) pay all outstanding taxes;
(f) pay all outstanding debts in full;
(g) settle all of the company's claims and debts;
(h) dispose of the remaining assets after the company's debts have been settled;
(i) represent the company in any civil litigation;
(j) produce the Liquidation Report and submit to the board of directors and competent approval authority for approval.

Liquidation Audits
Liquidation audits are generally required twice in the process:

- when the termination application is submitted to the related authorities and the application is approved by those authorities;
- when all termination procedures have been completed;

In addition to issues covered in normal audit procedures, liquidation audits focus on these additional issues.

1. The financial performance of the company for the 6 months before the date of declaring liquidation.
2. The completeness and truth of information on assets, such as

- whether the calculation of accounts receivable is correct;
- whether the bad debts write-off was properly authorized;
- whether bank account records are complete;
- whether physical assets properly belong to the company;
- whether disposal/loss of fixed assets is approved by the related authorities;
- whether investing assets are recorded and distributed correctly.
- the liabilities of the company, such as

  - whether salaries payable are calculated correctly;
  - whether tax payable has been cleared properly;
  - whether other liabilities have been cleared properly;
  - the liquidation expenses, and whether the liquidation expenses were spent in compliance with the law.

Liquidation Deadlines
The liquidation committee shall observe the following deadlines:

- within 7 days of beginning the liquidation, the relevant authorities must be notified;
- within 15 days of beginning the liquidation, the liquidation committee must be established;

2 Liquidating Joint Ventures

- within 10 days of establishing the liquidation committee, it must notify known creditors and ask them to declare their claims;
- within 10 days of establishing the liquidation committee, it must release an announcement in both a national newspaper and a local provincial or municipal newspaper. Within 60 days of establishing the liquidation committee, it shall make at least one additional public announcement;
- within 180 days of beginning the liquidation, the liquidation report must be submitted to the approving authority;
- within 10 days of submitting the liquidation report, the liquidation committee should perform the deregistration procedures with tax and customs authority and receive the corresponding statements.

Distribution of Liquidated Proceeds
In accordance with PRC Law, revenues from the sale or disposal of the liquidated assets shall be paid out in the following order:

- liquidation expenses, including expenses for management, sales and distribution for liquidation, expenses for announcement, lawsuit and arbitration, remuneration to members of and advisors to the liquidation committee and other expenses occurred during the liquidation;

  - wages, labor insurance premiums and welfare benefits of employees;
  - outstanding taxes;
  - outstanding secured debts;
  - other outstanding debts.

After payments have been made in accordance with the provisions above and upon completion of the liquidation procedures, the remaining revenue shall be distributed to the shareholders according to the ratio of capital contribution.

Cancellation of Registration
Upon completion of the liquidation procedures, the liquidation committee shall submit the Liquidation Report, approved by the board, to the approval authority, and return its business license and cancel its registration with the relevant government authorities including the MOFCOM, SAIC, the customs administration, the taxation authorities and SAFE. All the company's bank accounts shall be closed. The accounting books and other documents of the JV should be kept by the Chinese shareholder.

Within 10 days from submission of the Liquidation Report, the company should perform deregistration with the authorities, and upon completion of the deregistration, the company can repatriate the remaining funds back to the investor. The deregistration includes:

- deregistration from the MOCFCOM, and cancellation of the Approval Certificate;
- tax audit and deregistration from the local tax bureau;
- tax audit and deregistration from the state tax bureau;
- customs deregistration;

- deregistration with the State Administration of Foreign Exchange (SAFE);
- deregistration from the State Administration of Industry and Commerce (SAIC);
- deregistration of the Business Code Certificate;
- public announcement in a newspaper to terminate the business;
- remit funds back to investors;
- close bank accounts.

3 Converting a Chinese Company into a Foreign-Invested Enterprise

Valuing a JV Partner's Shares and Determining the Share Value
The Chinese government is taking further steps to try to prevent the dissipation of state assets into private hands at undervalued prices. These latter regulations have been tightened recently in the light of various scandals involving the cheap sale of state-owned assets to Chinese investors and are now quite stringent.

To purchase shares from a state-owned related enterprise, the share price has to be valued by a state asset appraisal firm which is allowed in this field by the government and approved by the pertinent state asset administration authority.

The price of shares should be settled based on the valuation result of the asset appraisal firm. So it is quite important who appoints the firm to conduct this valuation work.

There are two generally accepted approaches to valuing a business:

Assets-Based Approach

The nominated appraisal firm will conduct a thorough asset check of the company and determine the asset value based on the on-going operation assumption, and list all the debtors and creditors of the company. The value of the share transfer will be decided by the net asset value.

Income Approach

Valuations forecast the income or cash flows expected from the future operations of the business. These amounts often go forward 5–10 years. These amounts can then be applied to this method by discounting either the income or the cash flow back to the present value using appropriate capitalization rates.

Procedure to Complete Buy-Out

1. Hold a board meeting of the company to discuss the share transfer issue with the Chinese partner.

3 Converting a Chinese Company into a Foreign-Invested Enterprise

2. The Chinese partner, being a subsidiary of an SOE needs to apply for approval from its holding company and must file this with the SASAC.
3. Appoint an asset appraisal firm which can conduct state asset valuation.
4. Decide share transfer price base on the valuation report.
5. It may be required to hold a public action or bidding to finalize the share price.
6. Conclude a share transfer agreement between partners.
7. Hold another board meeting to pass the board resolution on share transfer.
8. Apply approval from MOFTEC on share transfer.
9. File the changes at the Administration of Industry and Commerce.
10. Payment of share price.
11. Financial statement and accounting record.

Two methods to settle the share transfer are

- payment of consideration settled in freely convertible currency from overseas;
- foreign investor may also use undistributed RMB dividends to settle the purchase.

Pre-application for New WFOE Name

If the company wants to change its name for the new WFOE, then it shall apply for a new name from the approval authority.

Approval from MOFCOM

Documents required:

- application letter to MOFCOM;
- board resolution on transfer share;
- agreement on share transfer between the two parties;
- new Articles of Association;
- new list of board members;
- passport or ID copy for all new board members;
- appointment letter to new board members;
- credit letter from the bank of the purchaser;
- notification for new name from the approval authority (if applicable).
- other documentations required by MOFCOM

Major Rules

- In cases of assets acquisition by foreign investors, the domestic enterprise selling assets shall continue to bear its existing creditor's rights and debts.
- A domestic firm selling its assets shall issue a notice to its creditors and publish advertisements indicating such in national Chinese language newspapers at least 15 days prior to the submission of the application for the assets acquisition to the approval authority.
- In cases where a foreign investor acquires a domestic enterprise in order to establish a FIE, the foreign investor shall pay all registered capital required in the acquisition to the shareholders transferring their share right or to the domestic enterprise selling its assets within 3 months upon the issuance of the business license of the foreign-invested enterprise. In cases where it is difficult

to make the full payment amount within the above 3 months, after approval, the investor shall make the payment within one year (60% within 6 months) starting from the day of issuance of the business license of the foreign-invested enterprise. The profits distribution will be based on the paid up capital ratio.

- In cases where there is a share right acquisition by a foreign investor and the FIE is to be formed after the acquisition, the investor shall specify within the contract and articles of association of the foreign-invested enterprise to be established, the period of capital contribution.

For share rights acquisition by a foreign investor, the investor shall submit the following documents to the examination and approval authority:

- resolution specifying unanimous agreement from the shareholders of the domestic limited liability company being acquired for share right acquisition by the foreign investor or resolution adopted by the general meeting of shareholders of the domestic limited liability company being acquired, giving consent to a share rights acquisition by a foreign investor;
- application for changing the domestic enterprise being acquired or establishing a foreign-invested enterprise according to law;
- contract and articles of association of the foreign-invested enterprise formed after acquisition;
- agreement specifying purchase of the share right of a domestic enterprise or subscription of increased investment of the domestic enterprise by a foreign investor;
- financial auditing report for the latest fiscal year of the domestic enterprise being acquired;
- notarized and certified incorporation/identification certificate of the investor as well as the credit certificate of the investor
- description about the enterprises invested in by the target domestic enterprise
- business license (duplicate) of the domestic enterprise being acquired and the enterprises invested by it;
- employee arrangement plan of the domestic enterprise being acquired.
- other documentations required by the relevant authorities

For assets acquisition by a foreign investor, the investor shall submit the following documents:

- resolution of the property rights holders or power of attorney of the domestic enterprise consenting to the sale of the assets
- application for establishment of a foreign-invested enterprise;
- contract and articles of association of the foreign-invested enterprise to be established;
- assets purchase agreement signed between the domestic enterprise and the foreign-invested enterprise to be set up, or assets purchase agreement signed between the foreign investor and domestic enterprise;
- articles of association and business license (duplicate) of the domestic enterprise being acquired;

3 Converting a Chinese Company into a Foreign-Invested Enterprise

- creditor notification issued by the target company and creditor's statement on the contemplated acquisition
- proof of identification or business opening and related credit proof of the investor;
- employee arrangement plan of the domestic enterprise being acquired.
- other documentations required by the relevant authorities

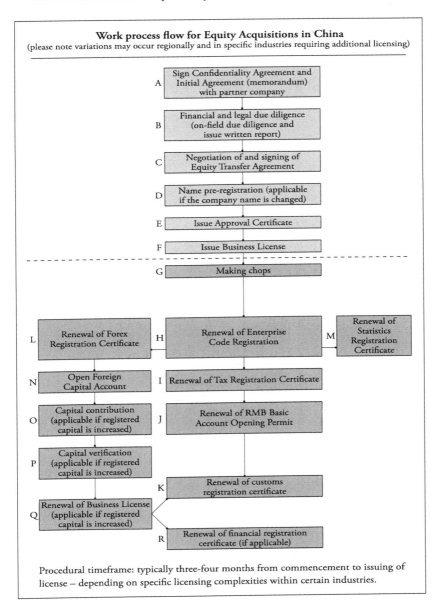

Common Mistakes

1 Common Mistakes When Buying a State-Owned Enterprise or Other Chinese Company

"It is the government so everything is OK." Actually this is not necessarily true, and in our experience, additional, not less, attention to detail needs to be put into effect when dealing with state-owned enterprises. Although the management of the enterprise may well stress "government connections", thus implying some sort of favored status, the role of the government typically ceases at the level of shareholders. It does not really extend far into management, except for businesses of extreme national importance, such as in energy or in the manufacturing of certain key commodities and supplies. For nonessential SOEs involved in various normal manufacturing and trading sectors in which the government has no particular vested interest, although the government will have a seat on the board, there is no guarantee that this actually manifests itself into anything meaningful within the operations of the business.

2 Cronyism Within SOEs

As mentioned, although the government may be shareholders in an SOE, the management of the venture has often placed themselves in positions to cement a regular income and to position themselves personally, rather than the government as shareholders, in taking advantage of any business opportunities that arise because of the existence of the business. The Chinese government has in fact had to go to extraordinary lengths over the past two decades to instill a sense of nationalism across the country, but in reality, many Chinese nationals still see the state as a provider and will exploit any business the state has for their own ends

C. Devonshire-Ellis et al. (eds.), *Mergers & Acquisitions in China*, China Briefing, DOI: 10.1007/978-3-642-14919-1_12, © Asia Briefing Ltd. 2011

104   Common Mistakes

rather than for the good of the shareholders. Consequently, with the government paying the bills in any event, the following scenarios are likely:

- sales/distribution relationships totally reliant on non-commercial activities, including the deliberate non-payment for goods or services received, or relationships that have been put in place on purely personal relationships first with any economic considerations being secondary;
- management in place that are ineffective and inefficient, with their sole interest being what they can take, rather than contribute to the business—and that includes your investment;
- other necessary operational issues such as sub-contractors, suppliers, distribution channels, and sales, that may exist within a framework that may not be included as part of the entity you imagine you are purchasing—thus ensuring you continue to be reliant on them even though you have purchased the manufacturing division.

3 When "Government" Ownership is not Government Controlled

As mentioned, we wish to be very clear on the point of SOEs and government connections. If mentioned, are these tangible or just being "sold" to you as a sort of assurance that "everything will be OK"? It is wise to remember that many of China's largest fraud cases have been where management of SOEs have deliberately sold out the company assets—buying them effectively from their own government—at a knock down price only to set up as a new, private firm, one month later, free of all liabilities and with millions of dollars of assets held privately that the state now does not possess. Yes, if uncovered, the government can and does sue. But when SOE management are fully capable of ripping off the state—what chance they will view your investment acquisition funding in a similar lamb to the slaughter fashion? And with local regulations and connections on their side, what chance of success do you have if you counter-attack and sue?

4 Due Diligence Issues

Consequently, thorough due diligence needs to be conducted on SOEs way beyond the normal legal and financial standards to establish that what you think you are buying is actually what you are getting. These include:

- *logistics, supply chain, customers and sales team.* Are you sure these are properly identified and included in the package?

- *land and other utilities.* Have you properly identified all land use rights and are satisfied that future access and the provision of utilities meet your expectations and are fully under your control?
- *environmental issues.* In China, the concept of "polluter pays" is in its infancy. If you inherit land that is polluted, you may face a clean-up bill later on from the very same people who sold you the land in the first place. Although you will need to go through the process of having core samples taken, and an expense will be incurred here, laboratories are close by in Hong Kong—and any pollutants found can be used to negotiate the price of the land downwards.
- *intellectual property.* Does the sale include the China IP, patents and trademarks of the business you are purchasing? Many Chinese brands are very valuable.

5 Other Due Diligence Issues

We have already touched on the importance of checking land use rights and licensing issues elsewhere in this book. Other legal due diligence matters should include catering for the existence of any outstanding legal matters, debts and other liabilities, and to have a letter of indemnity raised and signed off by the SOE protecting you against any actions made against the company for activities undertaken prior to your ownership.

6 Inheriting Employees

Employees are a huge issue and attention to detail needs to be put in here. Problems can arise such as:

- Does the company payroll match the numbers of actual employees?
- What is the status of part-time employees and do they have any claim on the company?
- What is the status and integrity of company funds such as labor union payments, and any other workers or other pertinent bonus funds?
- Are you 100% sure of the number and quality of staff that you will be inheriting?
- What are the pension and other mandatory welfare liabilities of any staff you inherit?
- If looking to downsize—what would be the costs?

Glossary of Terms

AIC	Administration of Industry and Commerce
BOFTEC	Bureau of Foreign Trade and Economic Co-operation (local approvals authority)
CIT	Corporate Income Tax
CJV	Co-operative Joint Venture
EPZ	Export Processing Zone (state level)
EJV	Equity Joint Venture
ETDZ	Economic and Technological Development Zone (state level)
FDI	Foreign Direct Investment
FICE	Foreign Invested Commercial Enterprise
FIE	Foreign Invested Enterprise
FTZ	Free Trade Zone (state level)
HIDZ	Hi-Tech Industrial Development Zone (state level)
IIT	Individual Income Tax
JV	Joint Venture
M&A	Merger and Acquisition
MOF	Ministry of Finance
NDRC	National Development and Reform Commission
PRC	People's Republic of China
RMB	Renminbi (Chinese currency unit, also know as Yuan or, colloquially, "kuai")

C. Devonshire-Ellis et al. (eds.), *Mergers & Acquisitions in China*, China Briefing,
DOI: 10.1007/978-3-642-14919-1, © Asia Briefing Ltd. 2011

RO	Representative Office
SAFE	State Administration of Foreign Exchange
SAIC	State Administration of Industry and Commerce
SAT	State Administration of Taxation
SETC	State Economic and Trade Commission
SEZ	Special Economic Zone (state level)
VAT	Value Added Tax
WFOE	Wholly Foreign Owned Enterprise (known colloquially as Woofies")
WTO	World Trade Organisation